On language char

In the twentieth century, linguistics has been dominated by two paradigms – those of Saussure and Chomsky. In both these philosophies of linguistics, language change was left aside as an unsolvable mystery which challenged theoretical entirety.

In *On Language Change* Rudi Keller reassesses language change and places it firmly back on the linguistics agenda. Based on the ideas of eighteenth- and nineteenth-century thinkers such as Mandeville, Smith and Menger, he demonstrates that language change can indeed be explained through the workings of an 'invisible hand'.

Refreshingly jargon-free, Keller's account of language change is comprehensive and clear. Not only does he provide a new epistemology for the science of language change, he also brings new insights to bear on the history of linguistics.

Rudi Keller is Professor of German and Linguistics at the University of Düsseldorf. He has published extensively in language and linguistics.

On language change

The invisible hand in language

Rudi Keller
Translated by Brigitte Nerlich

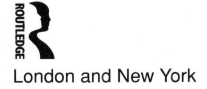

London and New York

First published 1994
by Routledge
11 New Fetter Lane, London EC4P 4EE

Simultaneously published in the USA and Canada
by Routledge
29 West 35th Street, New York, NY 10001

First published by Gunter Narr Verlag 1990

© 1994: Translation: Routledge

Typeset in Baskerville by
Ponting–Green Publishing Services, Chesham, Bucks
Printed and bound in Great Britain by
T.J. Press (Padstow) Ltd, Padstow, Cornwall

British Library Cataloguing-in-Publication Data
A catalogue record for this book is available from the
British Library.

Library of Congress Cataloging-in-Publication Data.
A catalog record for this book has been requested

ISBN 0–415–07671–4(hbk)   0–415–07672–2 (pbk)

It is more important that a proposition be interesting than that it be true. But of course a true proposition is more apt to be interesting than a false one.

(Whitehead 1933, p. 313)

Contents

Preface   ix

Part I Exposition of the problem

1 The problem of language change   3
  1.1 Why does language change?   3
  1.2 Organism or mechanism?   5
  1.3 Intentions, plans, and consciousness   9
  1.4 Essence, change, and genesis   13

2 Historical reconstruction   19
  2.1 The origin of language: a story and its interpretation 19
  2.2 Mandeville's paradox   30
  2.3 Conjectural History   35

3 In the prison of dichotomies   39
  3.1 Nature versus art – instinct versus reason   39
  3.2 Arguments in prison: Schleicher, Müller, Whitney 46
  3.3 Is language made by people?   54

Part II Solution and discussion

4 The working of the invisible hand   61
  4.1 Language – a phenomenon of the third kind   61
  4.2 Invisible-hand explanations   67
  4.3 Causal, final, and functional explanations   78
  4.4 Maxims of linguistic actions   90
  4.5 Stasis and dynamics of language   95

5 Discussion   108
   5.1 *Lüdtke's law of language change*   108
   5.2 *On the theory of naturalness*   114
   5.3 *Diachrony or synchrony?*   123
   5.4 *Chomsky's I-language*   126
   5.5 *Popper's World 3*   133

6 Conclusion   141
   6.1 *Language change as an evolutionary process*   141
   6.2 *Resumé and plea for explanatory adequacy*   152

   Notes   160
   References   170
   Index   178

Preface

I read Robert Nozick's book *Anarchy, State, and Utopia*, a work on political philosophy, more than ten years ago. It infected me with an idea with which I had previously been unfamiliar: the 'twin idea', as it was called by von Hayek, of spontaneous order and the invisible-hand theory.

'There is a certain lovely quality to explanations of this sort', noted Nozick. But it was not only the inherent intellectual beauty of this twin idea which attracted me; I also felt I was dealing with concepts developed by political philosophy and national economy that were just waiting to be adapted to linguistics.

Indeed, the transfer of this idea to the field of linguistics had been repeatedly and explicitly recommended by social philosophers and socio-evolutionary national economists for the past two centuries. But as the reading material of scholars is restricted by the structure of the universities and the boundaries between faculties, this offer had apparently never been taken up. This book represents the attempt to do so. It was my goal to develop and present a concept of language that does not neglect the fact that languages continuously change. If change truly is a fundamental characteristic of language, as has often been claimed in the past 200 years, it should be possible to demonstrate unmetaphorically why this is so. I do not intend to provide a survey of existing theories of language change; this has been already been done by others such as Lass (1980) and Aitchison (1991). Other authors' theories of language change are mentioned here only in relation to the theory presented in this book. The inclusion or exclusion of any such theory implies no value judgment. It is also not my aim to expound on the history of language; that here noted is employed exclusively in the explanation of the proposed theory.

To my knowledge, Noam Chomsky was the first to emphasise the claim that explanatory adequacy should be the goal of a theory of syntax. But what is true in the realm of syntax is true of all empirical theories. Such a theory should say not only what is the case, but also why it is the case. This book puts forward an evolutionary theory of language – the 'twin idea' of a concept of language plus its mode of explanation – which provides the framework in which linguistic phenomena should in principle be explainable, but in the strict sense, assuming that the necessary conditions are at hand.

I have tried to present the evolutionary concept of language systematically, interspersed with numerous examples of previous research in this field. To understand the solution to a problem, we must understand the problem that it claims to solve; to achieve this, it is useful to be aware of the failed attempts to reach such a solution and the reasons for their failure.

Students and the general public alike do not consider linguistics to be very entertaining. But this is a view that the object of linguistics – language and its historical evolution – does not deserve. When writing a book one normally has a certain audience in mind. The members of my target audience belong to three groups: interested laypersons, students, and experts. So as not to scare off the first two groups, I have tried to avoid a ponderous style and linguistic jargon. Where specialised knowledge is needed, it is introduced in the text and discussed. I have tried to present even complicated things in an uncomplicated way, but without radical simplifications; the reader will determine the measure of my success.

The thoughts presented here have evolved and matured over such a long period of time and have been discussed with so many people at conferences, talks, and seminars that I find it impossible to thank individually all those who deserve it. I can therefore only single out those to whom I owe special thanks. Erica C. García has closely followed the emergence of this theory with benevolent and helpful criticism. From the start, I got a specialist's understanding and support from Helmut Lüdtke. To Viktor Vanberg I am especially grateful for his critical comments concerning my former reflections on sociocultural evolution. Especially in the early phases of this work, Friedrich August von Hayek helped me to find my way through unknown territory with encouragement and countless bibliographical references. Roger Lass's comments on the problem of explanation and prognosis have provoked various modifications of earlier drafts of this text. I am indebted to Axel Bühler for countless critical comments on the manuscript. I would like to thank all of these very warmly. The original German edition of this book appeared in 1990. (Section 5.2 was written specially for the English edition and thus is not to be found in the German edition.) In the meantime, it has been well received, especially in German-speaking countries. English reviews were written by Peter Mühlhäusler, Raimo Anttila, Arleta Adamska-Sałaciak and Martti Nyman, whom I express my thanks, along with all other reviewers. Special thanks go also to the translator, Brigitte Nerlich, and to Hugh Murphy for his careful critique of the text. Kimberley Duenwald put the English version through a detailed final examination; I am grateful to her for countless stylistic improvements and clarifications. Also deserving of thanks are Rüdiger Wilke and Petra Radtke, who processed the text, and through whose critical attention a number of inconsistencies were prevented. Finally, I am grateful to Routledge for making the publication of the English edition possible.

I will not have exhausted this subject for a long time, and I will always be grateful for corrections, criticisms, and suggestions.

Part I

Exposition of the problem

Chapter 1

The problem of language change

1.1 WHY DOES LANGUAGE CHANGE?

In central Australia, where the rivers Murray and Darling meet, there lives a small group of aborigines who were forced to change their word for water nine times in five years, each time because the man had died whose name had been the accepted word for water while he was alive.[1]

We find it difficult to imagine such a situation. Australian aborigines, on the other hand, would probably find it difficult to understand why numerous people in Germany started to run after the English word *jogging* had come into fashion.

Whatever the case, these two examples show that a language has other uses besides the exchange of thoughts or the making of true statements about the world.

Languages are always changing. Twenty generations separate us from Chaucer. If we could board a time machine and visit him in the year 1390, we would have great difficulties in making ourselves understood – even roughly.

With Jane Austen, from whom we are separated by only 180 years, we would not have the same fundamental difficulties of mutual comprehension as with Chaucer, but we would hesitate quite often and ask for the meaning of a word. When Jane Austen described a man as being 'in person and *address* most truly the gentleman',[2] she was not referring to the 'gentleman's' residence, but rather admiring his bearing and deportment. We would not understand 'on the catch' or 'nuncheon'.[3] If a schoolboy wrote 'It is amazing*ly*'[4] in an essay today, it would be considered a grammatical mistake. To 'lay out a half-guinea'[5] meant, in Jane Austen's time, to *spend* a half-guinea, but it is no longer expressed in this way.

Even in newspapers and magazines from one generation ago, shortly after World War II, for example, some things strike us as decidedly odd today. 'What would an auto accident cost you?' is the wording of an insurance advertisement on page 37 of *Time* news magazine on 7 July 1947. Today we would write *car* accident. 'America's largest selling ale' appears on page 67 of the same edition. We would write *best* selling ale today.

Language has changed in the fashion world, too. 'Furs – A splendid collection at keenest prices' is how *haute coûture* described its wares to the wealthy in the (London) *Times* on 19 July 1950. Today we would write *a top-quality collection at competitive prices.* 'Neckties' have become 'ties', 'overcoats' simply 'coats'. In the property world, 'main bedrooms' and 'secondary bedrooms' have become just 'bedrooms'. It is anyone's guess how 'sufferers from the painful ailments in the rheumatic group can now obtain PROMPT relief' would sound in an advertisement today. The stilted style would certainly go.

In short, we find in newspapers printed about forty years ago a wide range of expressions that would be inappropriate nowadays in a similar context, although this varies slightly with the subject.

Why is this? Why does language change at all? Is the language of today not good enough as it is? Do you have anything to complain about, or do you want anything changed? No, in general, we are more suspicious of changes that have recently taken place than with the old ways of talking. Consider the uproar about sentences like *You need to know Spanish to fully understand Cervantes.* Ninety per cent of the English-speaking world does not know or care that *to fully understand* is a split infinitive. Quite a number among the other 10 per cent see this as a crass grammatical mistake and are not prepared to admit that it is, in this sentence at least, the most sensible word order.

This is just the same in the fashion world: novelties seem outlandish at first, but when they have become run of the mill, we just smile condescendingly at the previous version. This seems to be a universal game and a never-ending one at that. Could we imagine a language that does not change? Is this even a reasonable question? Instead, should we not ask ourselves if we could imagine a people that never changes its language? I shall come back to this alternative later.

Imagine for a moment that you are a linguist participating in the exploration of an unknown country. Would you expect to find a language that has remained the same throughout the ages? Surely not; but why not? Such a constant language would certainly have some advantages. Communication throughout the generations would be free of 'unnecessary' problems; the transmission of traditions would be easier; old people could not attribute their problems with the young to their language, and those theoreticians of language decay, as well as the purists, would have time to do more useful things.

But one can quite easily imagine a disadvantage, too: should the language of a people not keep in step with its social evolution? 'To cope linguistically with a world that is always changing, human beings need a vocabulary that is continually expanding.'[6] Is this really true? Let us play for a bit with our imagined scenario. Suppose you meet a tribe of people whose environment and civilisation had not changed as far back in history as one can look. Would you be justified in expecting to find that the language of these people had not changed either?

No, not even in this case. We can easily demonstrate this by looking at our own language.

What changes in our environment forced us to replace 'underpants' with 'briefs', 'cheap' with 'low-cost' and 'swell' with 'super'? On the other hand, we still use 'dashboard' for the panel in front of the driver inside a car, although it originally protected the coachman from the flying mud of the horse's hooves. To designate the departure time of an ocean liner today, we say it *sails* at such and such an hour, but no one expects to see sails hoisted.

Changes in our world are neither necessary nor sufficient to bring about changes in our language. The idea that this should be the case is part of the ideology which claims that language is supposed to represent the world (if possible unequivocally), and the task of communication is to make true statements about the world. But this is only one aspect of communication. To communicate means above all to have the intention to *exert an influence*.

1.2 ORGANISM OR MECHANISM?

One thing should have become clear by now: it is not as easy as it seems to ask the right questions about language change. However, in the formulation of theories, it is of the utmost importance to avoid from the start questions that could later lead one astray. 'Our questions fix the limits of our answers.'[7] The problem here is that perceptions and cognitive models which permeate the vocabulary of our everyday language are not adequate to describe processes of permanent change.

As far as I can make out, no linguist has ever had any doubt about the universality of change in natural languages. If it is right to say that *all* languages undergo continuous change, we also suspect that it is an *essential* attribute of natural languages to change all the time (although this does not necessarily follow!). 'That language undergoes continuous change is an inseparable part of its nature', wrote Hermann Paul.[8] But up to now, the arguments offered to explain why this is the case have been weak.

I shall come back to these arguments in more detail later. First, a word of warning about a fallacy: there are those who argue successfully that variability (i.e., changeability) is essential to language by putting forward the correct argument, for example, that this follows from its conventionality or arbitrariness. But they have proved neither that a language actually changes, nor that all languages actually change and even less that this should necessarily be the case. The facticity of change does not follow from its possibility, as do neither the universality nor the necessity of change. It is not a contradiction to say that although something is changeable, it has never changed. And it is no contradiction, either, to say that all languages are subject to permanent change, but that this is not necessarily the case (just as Coca-Cola is drunk in all industrialised nations, without this being an essential feature of industrialised nations).

Indeed, the **changeability of language** follows from its arbitrariness, which again follows from its conventionality. (If an equally good alternative for a certain form of behaviour did not exist, we would not call it conventional.[9])

The **universality of change** seems first and foremost to be an empirical statement.

The arguments for the **necessity of change** have yet to be discovered.

People have always found it very difficult, it seems, to understand processes of permanent change.[10] The reason for this probably lies in the fact that there are no obvious models of this type of change in ordinary life. We possess only concrete models of the process of *growth*: ontogenesis in living nature and the activity of the artisan. These have something in common. They are goal-orientated processes, those which presuppose the idea of a product before its completion. We shall see that both models have been used in linguistic theory.

The vocabulary of our ordinary language bears the stamp of these cognitive models. We have a vocabulary for creation and one for growth, but we lack one for evolution. What Konrad Lorenz said of biology applies just as well to linguistics:

> If we try to describe the process of global organic growth and at the same time do justice to nature, we always encounter obstacles, because the vocabulary of our language developed at a time when ontogenesis, the individual growth of living creatures, was the only kind of development known to man.[11]

The individual creative act of the artisan was the only means known to mankind of making non-natural products; the same could be said about the realm of culture. The words *development* and *evolution*' themselves evoke the idea of unpacking something, of the unfolding of something which already pre-exists in embryo, a conception which runs counter to the idea of evolution. (This might have been the reason why Darwin did not use the word *evolution* in the first edition of his work *The Origin of Species.*[12])

Either the processes of permanent change which could serve us as models take place too slowly to be observed during one life span, such as the evolution of animate nature, or we do not perceive the changes as processes of permanent change, although their speed in relation to our life span would allow this. This is true of changes in morals and customs, in religion, conceptions of beauty, and for the changes in language itself.

We usually regard these phenomena as cases of decay. They allow us to exercise our cultural pessimism.

It is sometimes claimed that human beings are not aware of the change in their language because it takes place too slowly and in steps that are much too small. Both claims are wrong. There are actually very fast and sudden changes. I believe that we do indeed notice language change, but that we do not perceive it as a permanent process. The typical way in which we perceive change in language seems to be as decay. Is it not odd that the various theoreticians of decay have been complaining for thousands of years about the decay of their respective mother tongues without ever having been able to show us a really decayed language? There also seems to be no one who is prepared to regret the decay of his or her own individual language: 'Oh dear, what dilapidated English I write compared to that of my grandparents!' Language decay is always perceived as a decay of others' language. This should make us suspicious.

In the matter of language change, we have a choice between two questions: 'Why does language change?' or 'Why do speakers change their language?' I shall call the first question the organismic version, the second the mechanistic one.

Both concepts have hidden traps. They invite us to give inappropriate answers.

Let us look at the organismic version first. Hypostatisations, metaphors, and anthropomorphisms are common in both scientific and ordinary language. We say of electricity that it runs, of genes that they are selfish; changes in air pressure are hypostatised as highs and lows which travel along, build up fronts, and are pushed back. These are convenient abbreviations. They are not problematic in so far as the respective experts, at least, have non-hypostatised, non-metaphorical, or non-anthropomorphic explanations available.

The question 'Why does language change?' presupposes that 'Language changes'. Particular to this hypostatisation is the fact that even the experts do not have at their disposal a solution which could be taken literally. We know, of course, that it is not the English language which does something when it changes. We know that this has something to do with the people who use it. But what?

History shows that the reification of language leads almost inevitably to its vitalisation. If language is indeed a thing, it is not a dead one, at least. Language lives. In it, forces are 'at work'[13]; it 'grows', 'alters', and 'dies'.[14] Again, the vitalisation of language openly invites its anthropomorphisation: the language 'searches for a solution', 'eradicates', 'seduces', 'fights for survival', and 'wins'.[15] As language does all this quite intelligently and skilfully, it ends up being provided with a 'spirit' (Grimm's *Sprachgeist*), which 'reigns' in it.[16] Thus, what was initially the basic communication form of *Homo sapiens sapiens* is unintentionally turned into an animal rationale with all sorts of wondrous capacities.[17]

The thesis that it is the speakers who change their language, presupposed by the mechanistic version of the question, is no less misleading. 'That is, have you or I "made" English?', asks Chomsky rhetorically.[18] My grandmother would certainly take the statement that she had changed the German language – even if only a little bit – as a reproach, and would reject it quite vehemently.

Both approaches to the question, organismic and mechanistic, have something misleading about them. 'Why does language change?' is too reifying, as if language were a thing with some vital inner force; an organism, as one used to say in the nineteenth century. 'Why do the speakers change their language?' sounds too active, too intentional, as if they had planned it and then set out to execute their plan; as if language were a man-made artefact, a mechanism that people could build and modify.

Both manners of speaking are fashioned in accordance with the two models of development mentioned above: ontogenesis and artisanship. Both are unsuitable as models for a language undergoing permanent change, and this essentially for three reasons:

1 Both ontogenesis and the activity of the artisan are goal-orientated; that is, the end product is genetically or conceptually anticipated. This is not the case in language.
2 Both ontogenesis and the activity of the artisan have an aim. (This follows from 1.) It is reached when the anticipated end-product has come into being. However, the 'life' of language is a potentially endless story.
3 Both ontogenesis and the activity of the artisan are individual processes. If an artefact cannot be produced by an individual, this has purely contingent reasons. Collectively goal-orientated actions are quasi-individual; in most cases there is a central planning instance to which the act can be attributed: 'Brunelleschi built the dome'. Both language change and biological evolution are collective phenomena. They are characterised by the fact that populations are involved in the process.

1.3 INTENTIONS, PLANS, AND CONSCIOUSNESS

Quite a number of people believe they know the solution to this riddle and set it out as follows: 'The 'mechanistic' version is naturally the correct one; it only needs some additional clarifications.' 'The speakers change their language' only sounds inappropriate because the speakers do not change their language intentionally and systematically but unconsciously.'

Would the following statement therefore be appropriate and correct?

1 'The speakers change their language, but unconsciously, not intentionally or according to a plan.

I think that this 'solution' creates more problems than it solves. The first problem arises from the fact that we are dealing with a collectivist statement. What does it mean to say that something is done unconsciously, when 350 million people are involved? What does each one as an individual do unconsciously? As long as the logic underlying the relation between a collective and its corres-pondent individual statement is not clarified, such a collective statement explains nothing.

The second problem arises from the fact that this statement contains three terms that are brought together in a rather con-fusing way. This terminological confusion has quite a tradition: **intentional**, **planned**, and **conscious** are lumped together. I would like to show that the above statement is unable to explain anything and turns out instead (when looked at more closely) to be empty and misleading.

Let us begin with the expression *intentional*. Theorists of action usually agree on the fact that actions are by necessity intentional. To interpret one's activity as an action is also to attribute intentions to one.

I think that this statement is true and ambiguous at the same time. It is ambiguous in so far as *one* can refer at the same time to 'person' and to 'activity'. This ambiguity is not a dangerous one, however, and this for the following reason.

An action has a purpose; a person has an intention (and not the other way around). To spell out the intention of an acting agent means at the same time to spell out the goal of his or her action. The intention of an agent is always to reach the goal of that action. (This is not a statement about the world, but about the semantics of the words *purpose* and *intention*!) That which counts as the achievement of the goal/purpose of an action is also the real-isation of the intention of the acting agent. Therefore nothing is changed by using intention where it can mean either that the intention of an action is its goal or the intention of an agent is the wish to do something.

There is another ambiguity, however, which *is* dangerous: the ambiguity of the word *intention*. It is because of this ambiguity that intentional is sometimes confused with *planned*.

The intention which is directed towards a future activity is not identical with the intention present when an action is executed. When I say *that* I have the intention to paint my garden fence next week, I do not say anything about the intention *with which* I want to paint the fence. I do not say anything about my purpose in doing so which will be served by my painting the fence.

I paint the fence in order to make it last longer. My intention today to paint the fence next week has no logical relation to my reason for painting the fence. In short, the intention *with* which something is done should not be confused with the intention *to do* something.

The intention to paint the fence can be either vague or irrevocable. The purpose served by my painting the fence can be neither vague nor irrevocable.

The intention to do something is a plan, and eventually an obligation one has laid upon oneself.

The intention with which an action is executed, however, concerns the logic of acting. An action is fully determined when the intended result and the intended consequence(s) of the action have been specified. However, an action is in no way characterised when it is said that its execution is intended.[19]

From now on, for clarity's sake, I will call *intention$_a$* (purpose) the intention *with* which something is done, and use *intention$_b$* (plan) for the intention *to do* something. We can therefore say that when we talk about the intentionality of an action, we have exclusively intention$_a$ in view. It may be interesting from a biographical point of view to know which of my intentions$_b$ I really put into action, but from the point of view of a theory of action, we only want to know about the intention$_a$ of my actions.

Mixing up these two types of intentions creates confusion. It does not follow from the fact that every action is by definition intentional$_a$ that every action has an intention$_b$. When I am about to open the door, I splay the thumb from the index finger to grasp the door handle. This action undoubtedly has a purpose. It is goal-directed, but I never plan to do it. The frequent claim that every action is planned, that there is a plan of action for every action, is based on a confusion between intention$_a$ and intention$_b$. This claim also leads straight into the disaster of an iterative regression: as planning is an action, it would follow that, if every action is planned, the planning itself should be planned, and thus also the planning of the planning and the planning of the planning of the planning, and so on. This argument is futile, of course. Theorists of action planning would deny that planning *in their sense* is an action.[20] But then they should also say what planning in their sense means.

Let us therefore keep the following in mind: the fact that something is intentional does not necessarily mean that it is planned. Language change could thus be intentional (which it is not!) without being planned. It could even be planned (which it sometimes is!) without being intentional. I shall come back to this point in section 4.4.

Intentional and *planned* are predicates which are independent of each other.

It is now time to turn to our third concept, **conscious** vs **unconscious**. The thesis according to which language change comes about not intentionally, but rather unconsciously, suggests a conflict. The assumption that intentional phenomena are also necessarily conscious phenomena is probably based on the lack of distinction in the use of intention$_a$ and intention$_b$, because everything that is intentional$_b$ is of necessity conscious. To have a plan means to intend to do something consciously. But not everything that I do intentionally$_a$ is done consciously.

We have a conscious awareness only of the general outline. We want to achieve a certain thing – open the door, go to work, paint the garden fence, and so on. These goals are all quite complex and we (normally) have a conscious awareness of them. However, there are many actions that are subordinated to them and of which we normally have no conscious awareness, although they too represent a form of intentional$_a$ actions, such as opening one's hand, taking one's foot off the accelerator, wiping the paint off the paint brush, and so on. We are all able to accomplish these actions blindly. As long as the use of the clutch, brakes, and steering wheel remain conscious actions, we are not good drivers.

It seems that in order to drive consciously we must be able to change gears unconsciously; to speak consciously, we have to be able to construct a relative clause unconsciously. We have to keep our consciousness free for the essentials of life.

Thus we continually accomplish intentional actions of which we have no conscious awareness. On the other hand, there are certain kinds of behaviour, such as ticks, which are not intentional, but of which we are consciously aware. I am normally aware of my blushing, trembling, or sneezing.

In short, *intentional* and *conscious* are also predicates which are independent of each other. *Intentional* (in the sense of *intentional$_a$*)

characterises an action from the point of view of the logic of actions, whereas *conscious* characterises an action from the psychological point of view.

The outcome of this discussion is the following: *Intentional* and *planned* are not synonyms; *intentional* and *unconscious* are not antonyms.

This turns our statement (1) into a simple list of negative properties. The speakers change their language neither intentionally, nor to a plan, nor consciously. This is generally true, and there is nothing more to it.

What we want to find is a positive answer to the questions of how and why our language, and possibly every language, is continually changed – perhaps necessarily – by its speakers.

1.4 ESSENCE, CHANGE, AND GENESIS

The problem may be formulated as follows: we communicate important things and trivial things, we use the written or spoken medium, we communicate in private or in public, etc. While doing so we think of the language as little as we think of inflation while shopping. By using our language, a million times a day, we change it continuously; or to use a more cautious turn of phrase, we produce a permanent change in our language. As a rule, we do not intend to do so. It leaves most of us indifferent. Most changes go unnoticed. We find some of them irritating or unpleasant, and consider others desirable; but in general, we cannot prevent a particular change, nor can we produce it on purpose. (I shall come back more specifically to the influence of language politics and language planning in section 4.4).

The question is, therefore, why we produce a change through our everyday acts of communication, and what the mechanisms underlying this continuous change are.

Traditionally, one factor – economising during articulation – was usually highlighted. But if this is the only factor that determines evolution, should languages not become more and more 'economical' with time, something which is obviously not the case (see section 4.5 and 5.1)?

If we knew what the mechanisms of linguistic change are, we would also know more about our daily success rate in communication, as we obviously communicate in such a way that the effect is a change in our means of communication.

1 If we knew what we use our language for, we would also know *why* language changes through communication.

The question as to how the process of change in our language takes place is therefore not an historical one, but a systematic one. The changes of tomorrow are the consequences of our acts of communication today. A theory of language change is thus at one and the same time a theory of the functions and principles of communication. (With this, I do not mean to contest the existence of non-functional random appearances in language.) Knowledge of the mechanisms of change has a functional–analytical aspect.

2 If we knew *why* our language changes all the time, we would also know *what* we use it *for*.

The second proposition is the inversion of the first. Knowing the function of an object is closely related to knowing *why* the object exists.

3 If we knew how communication functions, we would know something about the logic of the genesis of language.

A theory of the development of money implies a theory of the function of money.

This relation has a special significance for social institutions, although not necessarily so. An institution can have emerged from functions which are quite different from those which ensure its present continuation. It may be that the game called 'chess' emerged from a method for the simulation of battles. But when old functions have become obsolete, the institution in question need not necessarily perish; it can take on other functions. 'This relationship between the functional analysis of an item and a causal–genetic account of its existence, although often close . . . is by no means necessary', writes Edna Ullmann-Margalit.[21] All this should be seen as an attempt to preempt rash conclusions, not as an attempt to play down the relationship between a functional analysis and a theory of genesis. Such a relationship can be found in artefacts as well as in animate nature. Knowing the function of the purlin beneath the rafters of a roof also gives me a clue as to why it 'is there'. Knowing the function of a kidney (to use an example from Ullmann-Margalit) gives me a clue as to why it 'came into existence'. (I leave aside here the fundamental difference between the evolutionary development of the kidney and the manual

development of purlins.) This relationship is of seminal importance for social phenomena and institutions, such as law, money,
markets, morals, and language, assuming they are functional.
I would like to illustrate this with an example. In a photographic
series entitled 'Ten minutes in front of the Pompidou Centre', the
architect Hans Nickl[22] has recorded the genesis of a structure (Fig.
1.1). Curious onlookers form two circles on the square in front of
the Pompidou Centre in Paris in order to watch two groups of street
artists and travelling entertainers. We witness the documented
genesis of a very simple social structure. Just like the change of our
language, this structure comes into being without plan or previous
agreement; in other words, spontaneously. This is called a *spontaneous order*.[23] None of the onlookers intended the emergence of
this particular structure. Most of them will not even have noticed
that their actions contributed to the genesis of such a structure. For
most of them it will have been without importance.

I use this example to claim and exemplify that one cannot
understand the nature or essence of this social structure unless one
has understood the logic of its genesis. To understand this, it is
necessary to understand the function of the actions executed by the
participating individuals. A purely geometrical explanation of the
figure produced would not help to make it intelligible. The same
geometry could be produced by a company of soldiers who have
been ordered by their chief to form a circle of such and such a
diameter. The two structures – that in the photo and the fictional
one – could be geometrically identical, but they would be fundamentally different as social phenomena.

A structure such as the one in the photo seemingly comes into
being because everyone who contributes to its emergence chooses
a place according to the stipulation that he or she should

(a) see as much as possible,
(b) not expose him/herself,
(c) enable a certain number of other people to see as much as he or
    she does.

This much we have to know in order to understand this structure.
(Preschool children would probably only follow maxim (a), and
produce a very different structure, namely a tangle of human
bodies.)

An object (in the most general sense) is to its functions what an
action is to its goal, respectively to its intentions (the two should be

synonymous). To understand the structure generated by social phenomena such as this, it is thus essential to study the goals of the actions involved. At the same time, an understanding of the mode of production is a decided help towards understanding the structure itself.

This example is less suitable to demonstrate that such analysis of an action's goals is also an aid towards the understanding of change, since here we are dealing with a stable structure. But this means only that the action functions (a)–(c) create a structure which is (relatively) stable. If people followed maxim (a) *exclusively* (like the preschool children), a structure would be created that would manifest continuous change, namely a constant jostling forward.

I would like to stress quite firmly that I have dealt with only the functions of actions, not with the function of the circular structure,[24] and this with good reason. One could ascribe to the circular structure the function of giving a certain number of people a reasonably good view of things. But this correspondence between the function of the structure and the function of the actions that generate it, and where the structure meets the function of the actions, is not self-evident. The relative stability of the structure in this instance is due to the fact that, in this case, the correspondence is given. The example of the children's behaviour shows that it can be otherwise. Actions based exclusively on purpose (a) actually do *not* lead to a structure which would fulfil this goal. It is therefore unstable. Such a structure has properties that Friedrich Engels ascribes to history: 'What every single person wants is prevented by everyone else, and the result is something that no one wanted.'[25]

In the following chapters I would like to have a closer look at the connections between the questions about essence, genesis, and change in relation to language. I shall start, as one should, with the origin of language.

Chapter 2

Historical reconstruction

2.1 THE ORIGIN OF LANGUAGE: A STORY AND ITS INTERPRETATION

The Société de Linguistique de Paris, founded in 1865, made short shrift of a problem that had nagged the European philosophy of language for more than a hundred years by laying down in Article II of its statutes that no papers which dealt with the origin of language would be accepted.[1]

They had had enough of all the wild speculation *à la* Condillac, Süßmilch, Herder, and the rest. To share the prestige of the natural sciences, the linguists had to subscribe to the doctrine of empiricism. 'We have to investigate what is', said the president of the Philological Society of London, Alexander J. Ellis, in a programmatic speech in 1873.[2]

In the meantime, another century has gone by, and we can approach the problem of the so-called origin of language with a more open mind.

I would like to tell a story, the tale of an ape-man. The model for this story is Strecker's story about the small-world people.[3] What we are dealing with here is really something like a fairy tale, not the reconstruction of a past reality. The value of such a procedure will concern us later.

Once upon a time there was a group of ape-men. Ape-men are beings who have just passed beyond the stage of apehood, but who have not yet reached the stage where one could simply say they are human beings, because ape-men do not have a language. However, these ape-men had at their disposal, just like their closest relatives the man-apes, a rich repertoire of sound-expressions. The cholerics amongst them bickered and growled when they were angry; the boasters beat their chests and roared when they wanted to show off. They bared their teeth when they were amused, purred when comfortable, and gave ear-piercing cries when they were anxious.

All these utterances were far from being linguistic signs. They did not serve human communication in our modern sense, but were instead the natural expression of internal events; symptoms of emotional life, comparable to our cold sweat, or to laughter, tears or blushing. One does not communicate one's emotions with such phenomena, but they can, under certain circumstances, reveal something about them. Symptoms can cause effects similar to the way linguistic signs do.

One of the group was an ape-man who was rather disadvantaged by nature. He was smaller, more frail than the others and anxious on top of it.

We shall call him Charlie.

Being frail, Charlie was often forced from early childhood on-wards to be a bit smarter than the others. He had to compensate for his lack of bodily strength and his lower social status to avoid being completely and utterly dominated by the others. He was regularly driven away from the feeding place by the stronger members of the group, and they certainly never let him anywhere near the juicy bits. By being agile and quick-minded, he could overcome some of these obstacles.

One day something happened which was to be of immense importance for the future of the entire ape-mankind. The group was peacefully hanging around the feeding place, consuming the prey caught that day. As always, there were some minor scuffles and occasional pushing. Charlie was again shoved to the outer edge, where he discovered a pair of eyes in the undergrowth – those of a tiger. Their eyes met. Frightened to death, Charlie yelled in terror. The group dispersed instantly. Each one tried to find shelter in the next tree, because such a cry of anguish was the signal of acute danger. They had all been conditioned from infancy to react like this.

Charlie stood there as if frozen. Being so close to death had made him incapable of flight. However, to his great astonishment, the eyes of the tiger blinked at him in a very untigerly way, and their owner trotted off in irritation. What had looked like the eyes of a tiger belonged to a harmless bush pig. Charlie had fallen victim to his own vivid imagination, fed by his anxious nature.

But is 'victim' the right word here?

When Charlie looked around, puzzled, helpless, and rather ashamed, he saw that he was completely alone with all the food left behind by the others. The expression of fear on his face gave way to a thoughtful and even mischievous smile. He could not quite believe it.

Days and weeks went by, and every time the daily scuffle for the best bits of prey took place, he was tempted to do intentionally what had happened to him by accident.

What Charlie could not guess was that this temptation signalled the end of the paradise of natural communication. What had to happen finally happened. Again he had to watch how the fat bigwigs of the group distributed the best pieces among themselves, while he sat around hungry in powerless rage. That was when he succumbed to temptation. He emitted again the cry of anguish and again the group dispersed in a matter of seconds, including those disgusting bigwigs.

There they were, those little tidbits, loads of them. In his agitation, Charlie could not really savour them. (Perhaps his bad conscience prevented it, too.) But the first step had been made, and Charlie found it much easier the next time. In time he became quite ruthless. He took pleasure in his trick and began to overdo it.

As was inevitable, someone soon suspected him. When Charlie was foolish enough to yell for the second time during the same afternoon, one other ape stopped in his tracks after a few jumps, looked back and started to devour the food. Charlie was rather irritated, but not too bothered, because there was enough for two anyhow.

But soon the accessory started to use his knowledge, and, like Charlie, to exaggerate.

The number of those that saw through the deceit, and finally the number of imitators, took on inflationary dimensions. The community went through an extremely critical period. Everyone was suspicious of everyone else. The bigwigs tried to restore the old order by penalising every abuse of the cry of warning. But knowledge that has once been acquired can never be eradicated. On the contrary, it was reinforced by every new abuse and every attempt to penalise it.

The permanent abuse of the warning cry represented a danger to the physical existence of the whole group, given that blind trust of the yell of fear was necessary to survival. But those times were most definitely over.

Those who wanted to survive in those corrupt times had to have good ears. They had to learn how to differentiate between the genuine yell and the pretended one, something which did not prove too difficult for most of them.

As we know from personal experience and from dealing with young children, few things are more difficult than playing the hypocrite or attempting to express genuine feelings where there are none. The more ape-men learned to distinguish between the original and the fake, the less likely it became for Charlie's trick to succeed. Charlie was on the verge of giving it all up. Almost everyone knew now that Charlie's only intention in yelling was to drive the others away. Knowing this, they naturally checked out the scene first when they heard a cry before deciding to flee or to stay. At the same time, this knowledge opened up a totally new dimension in the ape-men's social life.

The breakdown of the ability to deceive with the cry of fear gave rise to the possibility of a new form of communication. Again, Charlie's contribution was essential.

As usual, the whole group had gathered at the feeding place to devour the results of hunting and gathering. Again, there was not enough for all of them. Those who were already fat sat in the middle and divided the food among themselves. They gracefully bestowed some of the inferior pieces on their wives, who had to feed themselves and the young ones, while the others had to be content with what they could snatch away. They could not expect the bigwigs to have any leftovers on a day like this. Charlie had stopped trying the trick with the cry of fear long ago. In an atmosphere as tense as on that day, he would have made himself even more unpopular than he already was. Besides, he would have attracted the others' attention unnecessarily. He had also learned that one had to proceed stealthily if one wanted to get something in a situation like this, by crawling up without attracting attention, making a quick grab and getting away.

The bigwigs could hardly cope with this gang of fast-moving thieves. You drove away one on the left and one on the right snatched something. Then it happened: quivering with rage and at the end of his tether, one of the bigwigs stood up, gave the gang of have-nots a sharp and menacing look – concentrating especially on Charlie – and bellowed the cry of fear. He who had never used the subterfuge before because he did not need to resort to it in his blind rage, making it clear to Charlie and his consorts that he wanted them to disappear.

He did not need to put a lot of care into uttering the cry correctly. Those who had so often succeeded in misleading him knew well what he intended. On the contrary, to fulfil its purpose, his cry had to be recognisable as only an imitation of the cry of fear. To invoke real fear in Charlie and the others was really not what he wanted to achieve. It had to be quite clear that the cry was not a reflex provoked by fear, but an expression of his will.

The cry of the bigwig was the first communicative action ever executed; the first utterance that was a case of communication in the full sense of the word. I admit that there was still a long way to go from the cry of the bigwig to a president's speech. But the most difficult step had been taken.

The story of Charlie does not claim to be realistic, but it says something about reality. It shows how the transition from natural to human communication *could* have happened. We are not dealing with a historical reconstruction, but with a philosophical one. Not the facts, but rather only the logical attributes of the story have to be correct. Some of them are that:

1 The steps leading from the natural cry of anguish to the intentional act should be plausible. The derivation should contain neither holes nor jumps.
2 The presuppositions concerning the abilities of the ape-men should be realistic. The story would be worthless if it attributed to Charlie an unrealistically high intellectual capacity.

Let us consider for a moment the intellectual problems that preoccupied those eighteenth-century philosophers who were concerned with the origin of language. Some of these problems are implicit to the formulation of the question for the prize essay posed by the Prussian Academy of Sciences in 1769. It reads as follows: 'If human beings are left to their natural faculties, are they in a position to invent language? And by which means will they achieve this invention on their own?'[4] Those who attempt to answer that question are lost. They are faced with the dilemma that Johann Peter Süβmilch had formulated so concisely in 1766:

Language is the means by which we reach the use of our reason; without language or other equivalent signs there is no reason. Anyone who wants to evoke the workings of the mind must be in possession of language. . . . Language, or the use of articulated

signs, is a product of the mind. ... Therefore he who first
invented language must already have been able to reason. If man
could be taken for the inventor of language, then he must have
been in possession of language before he invented it, . . . which is
patently impossible.[5]

Confronted with this dilemma, Süßmilch came to the conclusion
that language could only have been given to humans by God. To
think that language has no *origin*, but is only the result of an
evolutionary process, was impossible at the time of Süßmilch.
However, the question is not how a fully developed human being
can acquire a fully developed language, but how the animal
capacity for communication inherent in proto-humans could have
developed into the human capacity for communication.

Our tale shows a possible path from one to the other. We do not
have to claim that this is supposedly what happened or that there is
a certain probability. If it is logically possible that it could have
happened in this way, that is enough; in other words, if it is not
impossible.

But what do we mean by 'in this way'? It refers exclusively to the
succession of steps. In reality, the development spanned perhaps a
million years.

But is it enough to be able to reconstruct a possible logic in the
succession of steps?

A reconstruction of the logical steps in language evolution is
more than a theory of the *origin* of language. It is at one and the
same time a theory about the nature of language; a theory about
what we could call 'communication in the human sense'. Modern
anthropologists as well as eighteenth-century philosophers of language have always overlooked something in their reflections on the
origin of language: those who want to think about how or when
human beings could have come to have language in the human
sense must also think about what they want to accept as language in
our sense. It is not enough to examine the formation of the larynx
and measure brain volumes of proto- and early humans, and then
to ask if they might possibly have been able to speak. It can be
assumed that all animal creatures can communicate in one way or
another. More important is to show which way of communication
can be regarded as communication in the human sense.

'To communicate in the human sense' does not mean the same
as 'to have at one's disposal a language in the human sense'. The

ability to communicate logically precedes the possession of a language. A language facilitates communication, but it is not the condition of its possibility. To communicate with the help of conventional instruments such as linguistic ones is a special kind of communication, although this is for us the normal and prevailing way to communicate. We are so used to it that many think that the common possession of a stock of signs together with syntax is logically required (the condition of possibility) in order to communicate at all. If this were the case, we could neither meaningfully pose the question of how we as a species acquired language phylogenetically, nor how small children can learn their mother tongue ontogenetically. The reason is that the construction of rule hypotheses presupposes (among other things) successful communication.

The story of Charlie does not describe the emergence of a language, but rather the preconditions for it: the origin and nature of the ability to communicate in a human sense.

The genesis of these abilities goes through seven stages, which we shall examine one by one.

The first stage

Charlie, as well as the other members of the group, had the ability to produce a cry of anguish, but not the power freely to dispose of it. It was a reaction that followed the perception of danger. The ape-men could neither voluntarily produce it nor voluntarily suppress it (so as not to attract the attention of the enemy, for example).

The same goes for flight behaviour. This was a reaction following the perception of the cry of fear. The whole event had the character of a chain reaction: the perception of danger triggered the cry, and the perception of the cry triggered the flight behaviour. The cry was a natural sign, a symptom of fear; it was part of fear behaviour, just as sweating, urinating, or turning pale can, for example, be part of human fear behaviour.

The sequence of reactions leading from the perception of fear to flight is a typical example of natural communication processes, as they frequently occur in animate nature: two members of an animal species, A and B, communicate with one another if and only if A shows a type of behaviour that changes the probability of the occurrence of a certain type of behaviour in B.[6]

The probability of an ape-man's climbing up a tree as quickly as he can is changed by the cry of anguish: it becomes very high.

Contrary to communication in the human sense, the cry of fear was neither addressed to anyone, nor was it intended to be understood. It intended nothing at all.

The second stage

Charlie made a mistake. This can happen to anybody, and is not what matters here. What matters is that he realised that he had been mistaken and thus became aware that the cause for the flight behaviour of the others was not the danger but the cry. Up to that moment he, like all the others, had experienced the chain of danger–cry–flight as one complex whole, but now he realised two things:

1 I can scream even though there is no danger.
2 The flight behaviour of the others is the effect of the cry, not of the danger.

This is still only a hunch rather than a realisation. But this hunch initiates what linguists call 'displacement',[7] the ability to articulate an expression in the absence of its referent. Human babies, too, are unable to do this while pronouncing their first words. To produce a sound intentionally, it is necessary to realise two things. Those who consider it to be rather improbable that Charlie should have been able to make these two realisations at once can 'slow down' the story and start with Charlie making only the first realisation. Charlie could then repeat this realisation in play, and gradually approach the second realisation.

The third stage

Charlie exploited the two realisations. He produced the cry of fear with the intention of triggering flight behaviour in the others, so as to have the food for himself. This was the first time an ape-man carried out such an action. But it was far from being an act of communication. It is true that the action was intentional and goal-directed, and that it was thus closely comparable to an act of communication, but it did not aim at being understood; this is what distinguishes it from an act of communication. Charlie's action exemplifies the following scheme:

S does *a* with the intention
(1) of inducing reaction *r* in *H*.

In our scheme (1), nothing is said about the way in which the intended reaction comes about. In our scenario, we might suppose that flight behaviour is a conditioned reaction following the cry of fear. Human beings, too, sometimes act according to scheme (1): we clap our hands to scare away sparrows, for example, or we advertise something with a picture of a half-naked woman to attract attention to the advertisement.

The fourth stage

Charlie overdid the frequency of his deception and thereby started a process of blunting its effect. The conditioning is relaxed and a delayed reaction emerges. One does not flee blindly anymore. A moment of ascertainment splits the smooth chain reaction leading from the perception of the cry to flight. Related to this phenomenon is a big discovery, similar to Charlie's discovery in the second stage. Whoever refrains from fleeing blindly learns that flight is not triggered by a danger but by a cry, that danger and cry are not necessarily part of one undifferentiated situation. One discovers as a hearer what Charlie discovered as a speaker. Those two mutually related discoveries are decisive steps on the way from compulsive stimulus–response behaviour to free communicative action. They signal the liberation from the power of the stimulus. Freed from the compulsion to flee, one could soon use the trick oneself.

The fifth stage

Once someone has abstained from fleeing after the cry, the discovery of the freedom from stimulus will spread. The moment of ascertainment, the delayed reaction, will become the norm. In the end, the following will be true of every ape-man X and every ape-man Y:

Y knows that X imitates the cry of fear with the intention of triggering in Y the flight reaction, so as to chase him from the feeding place. X knows this about Y, too.

If X screams and Y does not flee, X will recognise with time that Y has seen through him; that is to say, that Y refrains from fleeing precisely because he knows that X has imitated the cry of fear, so as to induce Y to flee.

If Y has seen through X, and if X recognises this, X will also see through Y if Y tries to utilise the feint, and Y will recognise this as well. This is again a decisive step.

If we call 'p' the proposition '(that) the imitated cry of fear is there to induce the other to flee', we can represent the state of knowledge reached by X and Y in the following way:

1   X knows that p.
1' Y knows that p.
2   X knows that Y knows that p.
2' Y knows that X knows that p.
3   X knows that Y knows that X knows that p.
3' Y knows that X knows that Y knows that p.

Translated into the terms of our story, this means that everyone knows the feint (1 and 1'); everyone knows that the others also know the feint (2 and 2'); and everyone knows that he has been seen through by the others (3 and 3'). Such a structure of knowledge is called common or mutual knowledge.[8]

The sixth stage

As soon as the knowledge of the feint using the cry of fear became common knowledge, it became obsolete. This is when the story reaches a critical point. The group could have been doomed to destruction from now on, given that the natural warning mechanism did not function anymore. Another possibility is that the feint, once obsolete, could slowly have been forgotten again, and that the group would have regressed to its primitive communicative state. (In both cases we would never have heard anything about Charlie.)

In our story a certain differentiation took place. The majority learned to distinguish between the real and the simulated cries of fear. If now and then someone took the real for the simulated or the simulated for the real cry, it was irritating or deadly for the deceived one, but did not endanger the existence of the group. The stage during which the ability to imitate was exclusively used with the intention of deceiving could have lasted a long time. The ability itself is still remembered nowadays; we call it 'crying "wolf"'.

Knowledge of the ability to imitate the cry of anguish presumably brought with it heightened care on the part of the hearer. Hearers became listeners. This common knowledge also made it possible to move from the ability's manipulative exploitation to its communicative use.

The seventh stage

The seventh step is a tiny one, but it is decisive.

If I want to secretly tell my wife during a conference that I find it deadly boring, I can do this by turning to her and simulating a yawn. The simulation of the yawn has to fulfil two conditions:

1 It must be recognisable as a simulation of a *yawn*.
2 It must be recognisable as a *simulation* of a yawn.

This means it must be sufficiently similar to a real yawn and at the same time sufficiently different from it.

These were exactly the features (*mutatis mutandis*) of the bigwig's cry of 'fear'. The similarity of his cry with the real cry of fear made it clear *what* he intended to achieve (inducing the others to go away). The difference between his cry and the real cry of fear identified it as a simulation and thus made two things clear: (i) *that* he *intended* this effect; and (ii) *that* the others *should recognise* that he intended it.

The action of the bigwig is thus an example of the following schema:

S does *a* with the intention
(1) of inducing reaction *r* in *H*,
(2) of making clear to *H* that *S* intends (1), and
(3) of making clear to *H* that *S* wishes that *H*'s reason for doing *r* lies (at least in part) in *H* having recognised (1).

This is one of many versions of Grice's explication of 'utterer's meaning'. It defines what it means to communicate in a human sense. The execution of *a* represents an attempt by *S* to communicate with *H* if (and only if)[9] S tries to succeed in the intentions (1), (2), and (3).

This condition is fulfilled in the case of the bigwig's cry: he produced the simulated cry of anguish with the intention

1 of inducing Charlie to take off,
2 of making Charlie aware of the fact that he wants him to take off,

3 of making Charlie aware of the fact that his reason for taking off
should lie (at least in part) in this awareness (mentioned in 2).

Charlie understood the bigwig if and only if he recognised those
intentions.

If our attempt was successful, we have shown that it is not
impossible that the ability to communicate in the human sense
could have evolved step by step from the ability to communicate in
the animal sense.

Beyond this, we have shown what it means to communicate in a
human sense, and that this does not necessarily involve language.
The bigwig let his wish be known by non-conventional, iconic
means. Using a language means using conventional instruments to
convey to the other what one wants him or her to do. It is obvious
that these instruments can be completely iconic, partially iconic, or
totally non-iconic.

2.2 MANDEVILLE'S PARADOX

Our story has some paradoxical features. Should such a beneficial
and essentially cooperative institution as language have its origin in
the wish to cheat? Would not it be more plausible to assume that the
ability to speak had its origin in the wish to support and understand
one other, so as to optimise the success of the hunt, for example?[10]

'Among all living things, only man was given the gift of speech,
because only he was in need of it', wrote Dante in about 1305 in
his work *De vulgari eloquentia* ('On writing poetry in the mother
tongue'[11]).

Leibniz expressed a similar opinion in 1710. In his treatise for the
Berlin Academy, *De originibus gentium ductis potissimum ex indicio
linguarum* ('Short remarks on the origin of people, based mainly on
linguistic observation'), he wrote: 'I believe that we would indeed
never have created language if we had not had the wish to make
ourselves understood.'[12]

This has two snags, however: the wish, the necessity or the need
do not explain the possession. The wish to be able to fly does not
make wings grow, and the wish for eternal peace has led to a
number of wars. Beyond this, we will have to find a plausible way
that the *general* wish to make oneself understood could have
emerged without language.

In short, I believe that this initially plausible-looking approach rests on suppositions which are too complex. The force of an explanation increases with the sparseness of its presuppositions, and the story about Charlie presupposes only the wish to satisfy one's appetite. Besides, the story makes use of an old argumentative model, the structure and history of which I would like to present in more detail.

When we look at the world in which we live, we discover that there are people with highly developed technology and people with less well developed technology. A number of people use a hoe and manpower to work their fields; others use machines and tractors. Those with machines and tractors produce more and become richer than those with the hoe and manpower.

Now, one could argue that

1 There are those who are assiduous and those who are lazy. Those who are more assiduous try to achieve more; they develop machines and motors and thus, as an end result, become richer. Hence, their wealth is a result of their assiduity.

But one could also argue as follows (though I would like to add as a precaution that both arguments have only the character of a game here):

2 There are those who are assiduous and those who are lazy. Those who are lazy have always been too lazy to hoe and to use their muscles to work their fields. Their laziness drove them to invent all sorts of things that allowed them to reduce their workload. Hence, they developed machines and tractors, freeing them-selves completely of any work which depended on the strength of their muscles. Those who were assiduous, however, never shrank from lending a hand. Thus they have continued to hoe until the present day. Their poverty is a result of their assiduity, and the wealth of the others a result of their laziness. All in all, wealth and highly developed technology are the result of man's laziness.

What do argument 2 and the story about Charlie have in common? Three things: paradoxical structure, latent cynicism, and the strength of the argumentation.

Useful and positively valued social phenomena are explained as consequences of objectionable motives held by the members of the community. This is the paradox underlying this figure of thought. It turns into cynicism if we use it (incorrectly) in a prognostic way, and if we derive moral maxims from it. (If you want to get on in the world, you should be lazy, because the assiduous one will always stay poor.) The strength of the argument lies in the poverty of the premisses. The assumption that ape-men are selfish and gluttonous is simpler and more realistic than the assumption that they are helpful and unselfish. If one can explain a positive phenomenon even under the assumption that human beings act upon bad motives, one should choose this option. Should there be some good motives among them, they can do no harm.

This model of argumentation is called Mandeville's paradox. It is named after a man who has probably influenced European thought much more deeply than his degree of popularity would lead us to expect. Friedrich August von Hayek even attributes to him the fact that his reflections 'mark the definite breakthrough in modern thought of the twin ideas of evolution and of the spontaneous formation of an order'.[13]

Who was this man, and what is his contribution to the solution of our problems?

Bernard (de[14]) Mandeville was born in 1670 in or near Rotterdam, a descendant of a respected and prosperous family of Huguenots. In 1689 he received his doctorate in philosophy, and two years later in medicine, both at the university in Leiden.

In about 1696, he travelled to London to learn English. Three years later he married an Englishwoman and stayed in England until his death. He practised as a specialist of nervous and stomach diseases. In January 1733 he died in Hackney, London.

During his lifetime Mandeville wrote a considerable number of books and articles.[15] But in this context we are interested only in one: *The Fable of the Bees.*

What was to become a scandalous book had a rather harmless start. In 1705 there appeared a satire of contemporary English society, first as a sixpenny edition (and soon afterwards as a pirate edition), under the title *The Grumbling Hive: or, Knaves Turn'd Honest.* It was written in a lusty doggerel:

These Insects liv'd like Men, and all
Our Actions they perform'd in small.

This 'was probably little more than an exercise in the new language he had come to love and of which in so short a time he had acquired a remarkable mastery'.[16] The contents of the poem are quickly told. It was the moral of the story which was so explosive.

The beehive enjoyed power and affluence; commerce, arts, and sciences flourished, but among the citizens there was hardly one decent person. They were lazy and corrupt, vain and work-shy; there were 'Sharpers, Parasites, Pimps, Players, Pick-pockets, Coiners, Quacks, South-sayers'. The lawyers, the doctors, the soldiers, and the ministers were all, in a word, 'scoundrels'.

> All Trades and Places knew some Cheat,
> No Calling was without Deceit.

But the community flourished nevertheless.

> Thus every Part was full of Vice,
> Yet the whole Mass a Paradise.

For precisely these vices, at closer inspection, turned out to be 'the real driving force in commerce' and the reason for the general prosperity. In short:

> The worst of all the Multitude
> Did something for the Common Good.

This is the original form of Mandeville's paradox. The prosperity of the community was not the result of the virtue of its citizens, but of their vices and wickedness.

But the story goes on: when some of them went finally so far as to lodge a complaint with the gods about the vices of their fellow bees (while forgiving themselves their own vices quite gladly), Jupiter had had enough. He swore:

> ... He'd rid
> *The bawling Hive of Fraud*; and did.
> The very Moment it departs,
> And Honesty fills all their Hearts.

This, however, sealed the final downfall of the bee-community. The lawyers had nothing to do anymore; the blacksmiths and executioners became unemployed.

> Their Clergy rous'd from Laziness,
> Laid not their Charge on Journey-Bees.[17]

Commerce and trade were in ruins, until finally the beehive was reduced to a miserable, but 'exemplary and pure life' in a hollow tree.

Which so improv'd their Temperance;
That, to avoid Extravagance,
They flew into a hollow Tree,
Blest with Content and Honesty.

The moral of the story:

Then leave Complaints: Fools only strive
To make a Great an Honest Hive
T'enjoy the World's Conveniencies
Be fam'd in War, yet live in Ease,
Without great Vices, is a vain
EUTOPIA seated in the Brain.

And finally:

Bare Virtue can't make Nations live
In Splendor; they, that would revive
A Golden Age, must be as free,
For Acorns, as for Honesty.

In 1714, nine years after the publication of the poem, it was published again with additional comments on certain verses – comments which by far exceeded the volume of the original poem. Its new title was *The Fable of the Bees: or, Private Vices, Publick Benefits*. From that time onwards the text became very well known – in short, a scandal. In the following years, until 1732, it saw seven new editions, successively adorned with more and more additions. In 1729 the first volume was supplemented by a second, which appeared under the title *The Fable of the Bees, Part II. By the Author of the First.*

The whole thing now had the character of a socio-philosophical treatise, for which the original poem appeared to be only a pretext. The leitmotiv of the treatise was that every single vice, from drinking to vanity and laziness to whoring, made a beneficial contribution to the prosperity and well-being of the community.

This idea is really scandalous.

One can understand why a court of justice found in 1723 that 'these Principles having a direct Tendency to the Subversion of all Religion and Civil Government, our Duty to the *Almighty*, our Love to our *Country*'.[18]

What has all this to do with language and the theory of its origin and development? Later, the original paradox proved to be a special case of a much more general phenomenon. The discovery that morally objectionable endeavours of individuals can have perfectly favourable effects on society, that 'the individual's vice could mean the community's gain', was the germ from which sprang the insight that there are social phenomena which result from individuals' actions without being intended by them. What made Mandeville's thoughts so scandalous, the discovery of 'that force which would do evil evermore, and yet create the good', as Goethe put the paradox in his *Faust*,[19] played no role in the later philosophical exploitation, nor does it in the context of our study.

'Evil' actions can create 'good' structures, just as 'good' actions can create 'bad' structures. One example is the emergence of the inquisitorial practice of interrogation under torture, a result of the well-meant ban on sentencing people to death on circumstantial evidence alone. One can easily find examples for all sorts of combinations of 'good' and 'evil'.

What we can learn from the generalisation of Mandeville's paradox is 'that the question about the *motives* of individual actions must most definitely be separated from the question about the *social effects* of these actions.'[20]

In the story of Charlie this idea was kept in mind. It is of crucial importance for the theory of language.

2.3 CONJECTURAL HISTORY

'Mankind, in following the present sense of their minds, in striving to remove inconveniences, or to gain apparent and contiguous advantages, arrive at ends which even their imagination could not anticipate.' This was written in 1767 by Adam Ferguson,[21] a philosopher of the so-called Scottish School. The Scottish philosophers of that time deserve the credit for making Mandeville's idea the leitmotiv of their socio-philosophical reflections and elaborating on it with sufficient clarity. Ferguson continues: 'Every step and every movement of the multitude, even in what are termed enlightened ages, are made with equal blindness to the future; and nations stumble upon establishments, *which are indeed the result of human action, but not the execution of any human design.*'[22]

This is how Ferguson 'has provided not only the best brief statement of Mandeville's central problem', as von Hayek remarks, 'but also the best definition of the task of all social theory'.[23]

Leaving aside the tasks of other social theories, linguistics (if it is

to be understood as a social theory) fits von Hayek's assessment
perfectly: language is indeed 'the result of human action, but not
the execution of any human design'. The sense in which language
is such a phenomenon will be the subject of section 4.1.

Mandeville's fable of the bees has led not only to the discovery of
a domain of phenomena which many hold to be the object of social
sciences *par excellence*, but has also presented us with a mode of
explanation for such phenomena. Again, the moral philosophers
of the Scottish School were the ones responsible for the elaboration
of Mandeville's idea.

Dugald Stewart (1753–1828) reflected, like all philosophers of
the Scottish School, on the origin and dynamics of social institutions: if we compare the intellectual capacities, the customs and the
social institutions of our time with those of a savage tribe, writes
Stewart, we cannot avoid asking

> by what gradual steps the transition has been made from the
> first simple efforts of an uncultivated nature to a state of things
> so wonderfully artificial and complicated. Whence has arisen
> the systematical beauty which we admire in the structure of a
> cultivated language; ... Whence the origin of the different
> sciences and the different arts?[24]

To answer these kinds of questions, one cannot expect to glean
much information from history, which means that we are forced to
fill 'the place of fact by conjecture'. Although it is impossible for us
to reconstruct the process by which a certain phenomenon *has been
produced*, as Stewart goes on to say, it is often important to show how
it *could have been produced*. This certainly has some disadvantages,
because 'it is impossible to determine with certainty what the steps
were by which any particular language was formed'. But if we can
show, on the basis of our knowledge of the principles of human
nature, how the different parts of the language could gradually
have evolved, this would not only be intellectually satisfying, but
also a blow to that 'indolent philosophy' which tends to invoke a
miracle when it cannot provide an explanation. 'To this species of
philosophical investigation which has no appropriate name in our
language, I shall take the liberty of giving the title of *Theoretical*
or *Conjectural History.*'[25]

Conjectural History is not, as Dugald Stewart explicitly stresses,
an historical investigation, but a philosophical one. The story of
Charlie is Conjectural History, or, as one might say, a conjectural

story. It shows how the ability to communicate in a human sense could have arisen, demonstrated on the sole basis of properly attributed abilities, without calling upon God or a miracle. But the story of Charlie is a conjectural story of a special kind, as is *The Fable of the Bees*. They are special because of their type of explanandum. Both are conjectural stories about such 'institutions' which are – in Ferguson's words – the result of human action, but not the execution of any human design: the ability to communicate in one story, material wealth in the other.

Conjectural stories of this type are characterised by a certain twist. Let us look at the story which is presumably the best known of its kind, and which has given the genre of conjectural stories its name. It, too, was written by a moral philosopher of the Scottish School: Adam Smith. In his work *An Inquiry into the Nature and Causes of the Wealth of Nations*, published in 1776, Smith discusses the harmful effects of monopolies' privileges on the local economy. In this context he writes, among other things:

> But the annual revenue of every society is always precisely equal to the exchangeable value of the whole annual produce of its industry, or rather is precisely the same thing with that exchangeable value. As every individual, therefore, endeavours as much as he can both to employ his capital in the support of domestic industry, and so to direct that industry that its produce may be of the greatest value; every individual necessarily labours to render the annual revenue of the society as great as he can. He generally, indeed, neither intends to promote the public interest, nor knows how much he is promoting it. By preferring the support of domestic to that of foreign industry, he intends only his own security; and by directing that industry in such a manner as its produce may be of the greatest value, he intends only his own gain, and he is in this, as in many other cases, led by an invisible hand to promote an end which was no part of his intention.[26]

What we are dealing with here is, so to speak, a serious version of Mandeville's paradox. Whereas in *The Fable of the Bees* the vices of the individual are painted in caricatured exaggeration as the motives generating the public good, this function is fulfilled in Adam Smith by selfishness and the urge towards 'personal security'.

Without getting involved in a discussion about a free market economy, the *laissez-faire* doctrine and the evolutionary optimism discernible in the last sentence of the quote, I would like to clarify the underlying structure of Smith's argumentation:

1 Merchants commonly follow their own interests.
2 Every merchant will (if left to it by the state) invest his or her capital in such a way that it makes optimal profit with optimal security.
3 Optimal profit for each single merchant results necessarily in an optimal income for society, i.e., optimal wealth.

Premiss 1 is an assumption about the nature of human beings in general and about merchants in particular. Premiss 2 is a plausible hypothesis concerning the behaviour of individuals, based on the general premiss 1 about human nature and certain specific circumstances. Premiss 3 is a kind of 'projection' of the collective consequences, which would normally come about if the majority of the merchants acted according to the hypothetically assumed maxim 2.

On the whole, this is an explanation of the genesis of communal wealth and at the same time an explanation of nature and essence. This type of explanation is called, according to Smith's metaphor, an invisible-hand explanation. We can thus provide this provisional summary:

An invisible-hand explanation is a conjectural story of a phenomenon which is the result of human actions, but not the execution of any human design.

Chapter 3

In the prison of dichotomies

3.1 NATURE VERSUS ART – INSTINCT VERSUS REASON

One insight was always part of the discovery of such phenomena which are the result of human actions, but not the execution of any human design: that human languages belong to this domain of phenomena. This is also true for the *mode of explanation* of such phenomena, in the form of Conjectural History, or the explanation by the invisible hand. 'Of theories of this type economic theory, the theory of the market order of free human societies', writes Friedrich August von Hayek,

> is so far the only one which has been systematically developed over a long period and, *together with linguistics*, perhaps one of a very few which, because of the peculiar complexity of their subject, require such elaboration. Yet, though the whole of economic theory (and, I believe, of linguistic theory) may be interpreted as nothing else but an endeavour to reconstruct from regularities of the individual actions the character of the resulting order, it can hardly be said that economists are fully aware that this is what they are doing.[1]

One can rest assured that the last remark also applies to linguists. One can even say that the reflections of the Scottish moral philosophers were largely unknown to the linguists of the nineteenth and twentieth centuries. This is all the more astonishing as almost none of these philosophers failed to mention language explicitly. Is there an explanation for this oversight?

We live in a culture marked by dichotomies. Dichotomies determine our thinking: God and the devil, heaven and hell, good and bad, *langue* and *parole*, nature and art, emotion and intellect, and many more.

The dichotomies 'nature versus art' and 'instinct versus reason' have proved to be particular hindrances to the understanding of culture and language. The assumption that the world can be divided neatly into two completely separate categories, things which exist by nature on the one hand and things which are artificial, man-made, on the other, is as old as Occidental thought itself. It found its most concise philosophical expression in Plato's distinction between *physei* and *nomo* and/or in Aristotle's distinction between *physei* and *thesei*. It reappears in the dichotomic distinctions of the present day, such as 'natural language versus artificial language', 'natural facts versus institutional facts', and 'laws versus rules', to name just a few. Max Müller (1864) thus writes, for example: 'There are two great divisions of human knowledge, which, according to their subject matter, may be called *physical* and *historical*. Physical science deals with the works of God, historical science with the works of man.'[2] Henri Frei noted in 1929: 'La règle grammaticale n'a rien de commun avec la loi linguistique; la première est conventionelle (thesei on), la seconde naturelle (physei on).'[3]

The dichotomy 'nature versus art' is related to a parallel but no less misleading dichotomy: 'instinct versus reason' or 'emotion versus reason'. Just as one distinguishes on the level of objects between artefacts and natural phenomena, one distinguishes on the level of behaviour between behaviour guided by reason and behaviour guided by instinct or emotion. Thus the arguably most fantastic and certainly most decisive of human abilities goes by the wayside: the ability to establish customs or traditions and to behave according to rules.

What do I follow when I construct an English sentence correctly or shrink back from eating dog meat, or if I like to wear trousers rather than skirts, or if I prefer to sit on a chair rather than on the floor when I eat – my reason or my instinct? Neither! I follow traditions which have emerged in my country; I follow social rules.

'This false dichotomy between "natural" and "artificial"', writes von Hayek, 'as well as the similar and related one between 'feeling' and 'reason', is to a high degree responsible for the regrettable neglect of the essentially exosomatic process of cultural evolution which generates moral traditions [we can add here: as well as human language], which have determined the emergence of civilisation'.[4] In his essay 'Die überschätzte Vernunft', von Hayek demonstrates that reason and intelligence are not a precondition for the emergence of rule systems, but rather their effect. It is indeed the case that the human ability to act intelligently, systematically, and rationally presupposes the existence of systems of social rules. 'The true alternative to feeling is not reason, but the obeying of traditional rules, which are themselves not the product of reason.'[5]

One does not necessarily have to be clever to follow rules; nor does one have to contribute to the creation of customs. We do not follow rules because we know that it is reasonable or clever to do so. People follow rules because others do exactly the same. In general, we know nothing about either the usefulness or the function of a certain system of rules or a certain custom; nor can we think what would happen if we were to abolish it or replace one with another. The history of 'successful' missionary campaigns provides countless examples of the unforeseeable and often catastrophic results of 'rational' interventions in the primitive customs of so-called savages by so-called civilised people. 'Learning to behave in certain ways is not the result of understanding, but rather its source. Man acquires intelligence because there exist traditions which he can learn.'[6]

Rational behaviour has 'sight', but we follow rules 'blindly', as we do our instincts.[7] Social rules somehow become our second nature.[8] They are part of my ego. It is indeed rather difficult to decide in every case whether a certain kind of behaviour is guided by innate instincts or by rules acquired through socialisation. One has to have foresight to be able to act intelligently, because intelligence is the ability to solve problems without trying things out first. To follow rules, we do not need foresight. It is enough to look back and subsume a given problem under an already existing type.

Rules can justify our actions. But what justifies our rules? They do not need a justification, because they themselves represent the basis of justification and thus the basis of rational action. The ability to be guided by rules antedates the ability to be guided by reason, both phylogenetically and ontogenetically. Children develop rites and act according to them long before they are able to act rationally. Custom has its place between instinct and reason.

For what purpose do human beings have the ability to create customs? This question is wrongly posed. To those who have the ability – for whatever reason – it is useful. Part of the ability to create customs is the ability to learn behaviour patterns from your fellows which go beyond the innate patterns of reaction and behaviour,

behaving similarly to others in similar cases. 'The extensive pro-
longation of childhood and adolescence was perhaps the last
decisive step in biological evolution, until learned rules started to
predominate over innate reactions.'[9]

Incidentally, in a number of ideologically charged disputes,
it is often pretended that there is a question as to whether 'more
is innate' or 'more learned'. That is to say, one proceeds as if
one were dealing with an opposition in which a surplus on one
side would lead to a reduction on the other. This is not the way
things are.[10]

The reason for this is that every type of learning presupposes that
the ability to do so is innate. Even if one were to assume that the
ability to learn could itself be learned, we would ultimately have to
presuppose, for this acquired ability, an ability to learn which was
itself not learned.[11] 'The innate is not only what is not learned, but
what must be in existence before all individual learning, in order
to make learning possible', writes Konrad Lorenz.[12]

Let us return to the question of usefulness: how might human
beings have benefited from the development of the ability for rule-
governed behaviour? There are two answers to this question, a
general one and a more specific one.

Beginning with the general one, we can state that the three
types of ability, behaving according to instinct, to rules or to
reason, correspond to a living creature's speed of adaptation to a
changed environment.

The following passage, taken from Volker Beeh's work, makes
this clear. He demonstrates here what it means to behave:

As a borderline case of behaviour, one could try to imagine, for
example, a constant, rigid type of behaviour, as, for example,
perpetual motion. Irrespective of such behaviour ever having
existed, it is clear that one normally associates with the concept of
behaviour abilities of a type which allow the organism to initiate
certain processes relative to given environmental conditions.
The ability to do so must again be intrinsic to the organism, as the
delegation of the decision to the environment would in general
not be rewarding. Only such abilities offer a selective advantage
which, on the whole, make a choice that is favourable for the
organism. As the ratio of decisions made by the environment
alone to those that are at the same time favourable for a given
organism is normally low, only those species can survive which

take as many of these decisions as possible 'into their own hands'. The individuals belonging to these species must be equipped with an organisation which allows them to transform unfavourable situations into favourable ones.[13]

Our instincts represent such an organisation. It is, for example, very advantageous for human beings to close their eyes instinctively when flying objects come close to their faces. This instinctive behaviour was 'learned' by the species because individuals who in certain situations had a more pronounced ability to close their eyes had a higher probability of survival and/or reproduction than the others. This ability would thus more likely than not be transmitted to their offspring. What is innate on the level of the individual is in this sense 'learned' by the species. Processes of 'learning' of this type are very time-consuming. The time needed for a species to react genetically to a changed environment is hundreds of thousands of years.

Rules of social behaviour do not adapt to changed conditions overnight either. But the rate at which they change is very different indeed. Customs can change quite noticeably in the space of only ten or twenty years.

While instinctive and rule-governed behaviour is in principle conservative, this is not the case for actions guided by reason. Rational action is (in the ideal case) exclusively orientated by the logic of the problem that has to be solved, and not just by the way others solve it or 'how it has always been done'.

As the speed of adaptation to changed conditions becomes increasingly greater, it is set off by an increasingly greater lack of confirmation, which means higher risk. The repertory of instinctive behaviour has been tested millions of times and has been well established for thousands of years. It is inflexible, but it is totally reliable. Rule-governed behaviour, too, is sometimes tested millions of times and well established for tens or hundreds of years. It is of medium flexibility, so to speak, with medium reliability. It combines behavioural stereotypes with relatively high reliability.

Rational behaviour is, by contrast, highly risky. It allows complete adaptation to any new condition, but carries the full risk of failure. Doing the wrong thing in a big way is the privilege of human beings, because the prerequisite is the ability to act according to reason.

To the question about rule-governed behaviour's usefulness for human beings, our general answer is therefore that it allows us to react to problems in a more flexible and more specific way than the instinctive repertory of behaviour would.

Let us look at a more specific answer to this question. In his already mentioned essay 'Die überschätzte Vernunft', von Hayek proposes the following:

> The innate instincts of man are not made for a society such as the one he lives in today. These instincts were adapted to life in small groups in which he found himself during the millennia of human evolution. . . . The extended society is a result of the evolution of certain traditional rules of behaviour which quite often told him not to do what his instincts urged him to do.[14]

In short, the usefulness of emerged systems of social rules lay in the fact that they made it possible to create large societies.

As it seems quite plausible to me, I would like to speculate further on von Hayek's approach. Above all, I would like to exploit it for the analysis of language.

Compared to small communities, large societies have the advantage of having at their disposal a plethora of knowledge and abilities far beyond the capacity of each individual member. In conjunction with the principle of the division of labour, this allows the individual members of such a society to enjoy goods, standards, and abilities which they would never be able to produce as individuals or in small groups.[15] But it must be stressed that life in a large society requires completely different forms of social behaviour. Life in the smaller communities was characterised by 'a strictly limited co-operation between individuals who knew each other, guided by the joint perception of events, visible to all, and recognised by all as a potential source of food or danger'.[16] The power structure inside the communities probably had the form of a pecking order, established on each occasion according to the rule of power to the strongest.

In order to form larger societies, the principle of co-existence based on a concrete goal visible to all, along with the rule of power to the strongest, must be replaced by more abstract principles and rules of behaviour. Custom is the primitive form, so to speak, of more abstract principles of action. To act according to a custom in a given situation means generalising from the concrete case and subsuming it under a type where 'one' behaves in this or that way.

A language is a custom; by now, a gigantic one that allows us to bring about certain things.

For a larger society to emerge, it is necessary to regulate violence or to replace violence by peaceful alternatives. The fundamental institutions which are substitutes for violence are law, markets, and language. This combination may seem bizarre at first glance. I shall leave open the question of whether language has a certain priority, as Adam Smith suspects in the second chapter of *The Wealth of Nations*, and explain what is common to these three 'customs'.

The custom of law has the function of assigning the regulation of conflicts to a third (neutral) party. The individual abandons the right to retaliation to a party or institution, which in turn provides protection against unreasonable, unjust, and undeserved acts of retaliation by others. The law is thus barter: I give my right to revenge to a third party or institution (a state, a chief, the mafia, or something of that kind), and in return I receive protection against the arbitrary actions of others.

Market and language serve related purposes. Both are institutions which help to get someone else to do a certain thing. The market is the institution I use when I want to get someone to give me a certain thing; language is the institution I use if I want to get someone to do something or to believe a certain thing.

The archaic alternative to markets and language is violence; to trade, it is robbery or theft; to communication, force.

In simple terms, to trade means to give someone, who has what one needs and needs what one has, that which one has, so as to get what one needs.

To communicate means, in simple terms, to make one's wishes and convictions known to someone else, in the hope and with the intention that this might be a reason for the other to fulfil one's wish or adopt one's conviction.

Communication and trade are based on the same principle: if you want to get others to do a certain thing, give them a reason to do it on their own behalf. To get what I need is sometimes a good reason for me to give you something that you want from what I have. To find out that you believe something is true is sometimes a good reason for me to believe this as well. To know that you want me to do a certain thing can sometimes be a good reason for me to do it.

Buying something with money is a particular case of the actions described here in general. Money is a conventional means to speed up the transaction. It shortens my search for someone who has what

I need and needs what I have, because money is something that almost everyone needs.

Communication by language, too, is a particular case of the communication process described here in general. Language is a conventional means to speed up the transaction, to refine it, and very often to make it at all possible. It facilitates or makes it possible to let others know what one would like to have them do.

I admit that the last two sentences hide a dangerous shortcut if they are to be applied to our present, fully developed language. Language has become autonomous (as, incidentally, has the market economy), so that an instrumentalist perspective falls short of capturing its true essence. A comparison might make this clearer.

'Chess is a conventional means to checkmate someone.' What is odd about this statement? It takes an improperly instrumentalist perspective. The relation between chess and checkmate is different, for example, from that between a drill and a hole, because the existence of holes is logically independent of the existence of drills, and 'hole' can be defined without using 'drill' in the definition. Fully developed languages, like modern human languages, are therefore, strictly speaking, not only good instruments with which to do certain things. They constitute precisely those things one can do with them, just as the game of chess constitutes checkmate.

Let us return to the dichotomy discussed at the beginning of this chapter, that of 'art versus nature'. In the nineteenth century, linguists were virtually fixated on this dichotomy. The result was that, despite all their strenuous efforts, they could never develop a concept of language that was adequate to language. In the following section I would like to describe this fixation by means of examples.

3.2 ARGUMENTS IN PRISON: SCHLEICHER, MÜLLER, WHITNEY

'The Greek dichotomy which had governed thinking so long, and which still has not lost all its power, is that between what is natural (*physei*) and that which is artificial or conventional (*thesei* or *nomo*).' It became, according to von Hayek, 'so firm a tradition that it acted like a prison from which Mandeville at last showed the way of escape'.[17]

As the great majority of linguists had overlooked this escape route, they remained for a long time victims of their own self-imposed limitations.

With the help of arguments taken from August Schleicher, Max Müller, and William Dwight Whitney, I would like to show the kind of limitations they were dealing with.

In the nineteenth century, the leitmotiv of many sciences was the search for laws of development. Charles Lyell, Herbert Spencer, Charles Darwin, and Karl Marx all participated in this search, each according to the framework of his respective discipline; the success of this search is still a matter of debate, as we know. The efforts of the linguists were in any case quite respectable. Comparative linguistics had brought to light a number of the Indo-European languages' *Lautgesetze*. Through backward extrapolation of the discovered regularities, it was thought possible to reconstruct the Indo-European *Ursprache* or proto-language.

In 1868, August Schleicher published a little fable in this language. 'In part to demonstrate that one can, although laboriously, construct coherent sentences in the Indo-European proto-language, I made the attempt, in part simply *animi causa*, to write some lines in this reconstructed language.'[18]

Avis, jasmin varná na á ast, dadarka akvams, tam, vágham garum vaghantam, tam, bháram, tam, manum áku bharantam. Avis akvbhjams á vavakat: kard aghnutai mai vidanti manum akvams agantam.

[A] sheep, [on] which wool not was saw horses, this [a] heavy cart pulling, this [a] big load, this [a] man carrying quickly. [The] sheep said [to the] horses: [The] heart is [in] me narrow, seeing [the] man [the] horses flogging.

From a modern point of view this is evidently witty nonsense. It is clear that a comparative method does not necessarily lead to the original forms. It is based on the completely unfounded premiss that something common to two (or more) things is also their source. Besides, the hypothesis that all Indo-European languages developed from a single root language is completely unfounded.

Be this as it may, there was general agreement about the fact that languages develop, not only continuously, but also necessarily. However, there was disagreement about the question of why this should be so; linguists disagreed about the ontological status, the nature of language. Naturally linked to the first was another source of disagreement, concerning the status of the discovered regularities in the development.

In his treatise 'Darwinism Tested by the Science of Language', Schleicher put forth an extreme, but therefore also very clear, point of view:

> Languages are organisms of nature; they have never been directed by the will of man; they rose, and developed themselves according to definite laws; they grew old, and died out. They, too, are subject to that series of phenomena which we embrace under the name of 'life'. The science of language is consequently a natural science; its method is generally altogether the same as that of any other natural science.[19]

How could Schleicher have been so sure about this? 'Observation is the foundation of modern knowledge.'[20] It is because linguistics, like biology, is a natural science, and 'nothing is of any importance to science but such *facts* as have been established by close objective observation, and the proper conclusions derived from them'.[21]

A modern reader can only wonder at the epistemological naivety of such a great scholar. How little 'strictly objective observation' can protect against errors! Whitney was one of the first to notice the discrepancy between Schleicher's scientific achievements and his epistemological views:

> The name of August Schleicher cannot be uttered by any student of comparative philology of the present generation without respect and admiration. . . . There is, unfortunately, no necessary connection between eminence in one of these characters and in the other; many a great comparative philologist has either left untouched the principles and laws underlying the phenomena with which he deals, or has held respecting them views wholly superficial, or even preposterous and absurd.[22]

Schleicher's nonsensical views about the nature of language were surely motivated by the deep wish to be allowed to participate in the prestige of the successful natural sciences. At that time, this wish was widely shared (and has not quite disappeared in our time). 'The natural sciences ride triumphantly in the chariot of victory to which we are all chained', wrote the linguist Wilhelm Scherer.[23]

Perhaps he should have written 'onto which we all want to jump'.

Schleicher used a simple trick to transform linguistics into a natural science. He took the metaphor of language-as-organism literally, and then drew his own conclusions. 'Now observation teaches us that all living organisms . . . vary according to definite laws',[24] and it teaches us this with 'a most positive certainty'.[25] He tried to further support the thesis of linguistics' link to natural science by showing similarities between it and 'Darwinian theory'.[26] He believed, for example, that 'the simple cell is, no doubt, the common primitive form of those [organisms], as the simple root is that of the languages',[27] and 'Where we are sufficiently familiar with any particular family of speech we draw up a genealogical table similar to the one which Darwin attempted for the species of animals and plants.'[28]

But there is not much of Darwin's spirit in Schleicher, who would have liked so much to participate in his glory. He (and with him all those who continue to call him a Darwinist today) completely overlooked, for example, that his comparison between the 'life' of a language and the growth, ageing and death of a plant is not an example of Darwinism, but an ineffective attempt to conceive the evolutionary process as an ontogenetic one. He would not have had to wait for Darwin to find this comparison. The growth, life, and death of a living creature does not have any significant similarity to the metaphorical 'life of a linguistic organism'.

What made Schleicher think that a linguistic organism (to continue with the language of the time) should be a *natural* organism? 'Organism' did not mean 'natural organism' *per se* at that time. Humboldt, for example, did not leave any doubt that linguistic organisms can exist only in and through the human being. Schleicher used a criterion accepted equally by supporters and opponents of his conception: *the dependence on or the independence from the human will* was seen as the decisive factor that determined the naturalness or artificiality of a phenomenon.

Characteristic of natural organisms is that they evolve without being 'directed by the will of man'.[29] The evolution of a language cannot be determined by the will of man. Therefore, language is a natural organism and its science is a natural science.

This is the structure of the argument whose most essential weakness lies in the highest premiss. It is imprisoned in the dichotomy of nature and art.

It is instructive to look at Max Müller's argumentation concerning this topic. During the last third of the nineteenth century, he was one of the world's best-known linguists. He lived in Oxford and was an important Sanskritologist, having edited and translated the Righveda, although his fame in Europe and the United States was mostly a result of his ability to present the state of contemporary linguistics in a popular, pleasant, and readable form. The 'Lectures on Language', presented in the years 1861 and 1863 at the Royal Institute of London, were a best-seller and translated into many languages.

To anticipate the punch line of the story: Müller arrived at a result similar to Schleicher's, though his arguments were subtler. He even criticised Schleicher's form of argument, because he recognised how weak it was:

> If we must compare language with a tree, there is one point which may be illustrated by this comparison, and this is that neither language nor the tree can exist or grow by itself. Without the soil, without air and light, the tree could not live; it could not even be conceived to live. It is the same with language. Language cannot exist by itself; it requires a soil on which to grow, and that soil is the human soul. To speak of language as a thing by itself, as living a life of its own, as growing to maturity, producing offspring, and dying away, is sheer mythology; and though we cannot help using metaphorical expressions, we should always be on our guard, when engaged in inquiries like the present, against being carried away by the very words we are using.[30]

One can fully agree with this, but it does not constitute too great a concession on the part of someone who – as he said – 'always took it for granted that the science of language . . . is one of the physical sciences, and therefore its method ought to be the same as that which has been followed with so much success in botany, geology, anatomy, and other branches of the study of nature.'[31]

Does it not seem necessary to count linguistics among the 'historical sciences' which deal 'with the works of man'? Is it not true that the 'physical sciences', that is, the 'natural sciences', deal 'with the works of God'?[32] But Müller even dared to go a step further: not even the Bible claims that language is a work of God! 'For in the Bible it is not the Creator who gives names to all things, but Adam.'[33]

Indeed, everything speaks against counting linguistics as a natural science and everything in favour of it being a 'historical science'. One should also keep in mind that language undergoes historical changes. 'The historical changes of language may be more or less rapid, but they take place at all times and in all countries.'[34]

How did Müller escape from this argumentational cul-de-sac? 'In claiming for the science of language a place among the physical sciences, I was prepared to meet with many objections.'[35] His central argument was as follows:

> It is argued, therefore, that as language, differing thereby from all other productions of nature, is liable to historical alterations, it is not fit to be treated in the same manner as the subject-matter of all the other physical sciences.
> There is something very plausible in this objection, but if we examine it more carefully, we shall find *that it rests entirely on a confusion of terms.* We must distinguish between historical change and natural growth. Art, science, philosophy, and religion all have a history; language, or any other production of nature, admits only of growth.[36]

The concept of growth seems to have played a central role in England at the time Müller was writing. Herbert Spencer notes, for example, in Chapter III of his 1864 work *Principles of Biology,* 'that societies are not made but *grow*'.[37]

What criterion did Müller use to distinguish between history and growth? It is our by now familiar criterion of voluntary determination through man:

> Let us consider, first, that although there is a continuous change in language, it is not in the power of man either to produce or to prevent it. We might think as well of changing the laws which control the circulation of our blood, or of adding an inch to our height, as of altering the laws of speech, or inventing new words according to our own pleasure.[38]

Hence language is a natural phenomenon. Here we have it again – the argument inside the prison of the natural–artificial dichotomy. It goes without saying that there was also a different position, the complementary one. William D. Whitney was one of its proponents. According to him, linguistics is 'one of the most prestigious of the historical or moral[39] sciences [*Geisteswissenschaften*]'.[40]

Why should this be the case? The criterion remains the same.

We must not fail to appreciate the essential difference between the material of the physical siences and that of our subject; that we have to deal with the usages of man, in all of which inter-

venes that indefinite element, the human will as determined by
circumstance, by habit, by individual character.[41]

As a direct answer to Schleicher's remark that languages are not
determined by the will of man, Whitney wrote:

> If the voluntary action of man has anything to do with making
> and changing language, then language is so far not a natural
> organism, but a human product. And if that action is the only
> force that makes and changes language, then language is not a
> natural organism at all, nor its study a natural science.[42]

Whitney's cautious choice of words is remarkable. He did not
claim that human beings make their language and change it, but
that voluntary actions 'have something to do with it', or that
action 'is the only force'. This mode of expression would be quite
compatible with the thesis that language is the result of human
action, but not the execution of any human design. Indeed,
Whitney came very close to this view in his writing. But when we
read 'of somewhat the same character is a Beethoven symphony, a
Greek temple, an Egyptian pyramid',[43] we realise that the distinction between an artefact and a so-called natural language was not
recognised by Whitney. He looked in the right direction when
trying to find a way out of the prison, something well demonstrated
by his choice of the concept of institution. 'If we are to give
language a name which shall bring out its essential character most
distinctly and sharply . . ., we shall call it an INSTITUTION, one of the
institutions that make up human culture.'[44]

But if the nature of language had been as clear to him as he
alleged it was, and as it sometimes seems to be, he would certainly
have noticed that a symphony, a temple, or a pyramid are not
institutions in this sense.

To conclude, let us look at all three authors again: Schleicher,
Müller, and Whitney. What is common to them and what distinguishes them from one another?

Schleicher and Müller regarded language as a natural phenomenon; Whitney saw it as a cultural phenomenon. For Schleicher,
everything was crystal clear: language is a natural organism;
organisms live and die; whatever lives and dies is part of nature.
Linguistics is, therefore, a natural science. Schleicher defended
this position stubbornly, without any ifs or buts. In the final
analysis, Müller came to the same conclusion, but he clearly felt

uneasy about it. Whitney arrived at an opposite result, and was not quite comfortable with it either. It is surprising to find passages from the two authors that are not only similar, but which indicate quite clearly Mandeville's escape route from the prison. Max Müller wrote:

The process through which language is settled and unsettled combines in one the two opposite elements of *necessity and free will*. Though the individual seems to be the prime agent in producing new words and new grammatical forms, he is so only after his individuality has been merged in the common action of the family, tribe or nation to which he belongs. . . . The individual, as such, is powerless, and the results apparently produced by him depend on laws beyond his control, and on the cooperation of all those who form together with him one class, one body, or one organic whole.[45]

One can sense the effort to find a way out, an approach to the idea that a language is the unintentional collective result of intentional actions by individuals. His reflections aim in the right direction, but he was unable to divest himself completely of the vitalistic inheritance of Schleicher. However, his observation that the development of a language is due to the joint effect of free will and necessity is noteworthy. We shall have to return to this aspect! The corresponding passage from Whitney reads as follows:

The desire of communication is a real living force, to the impelling action of which every human being, in every stage of culture, is accessible; and so far as we can see, it is the only force that was equal to initiating the process of language-making, as it is also the one that has kept up the process to the present time. It works both consciously and unconsciously, as regards the further consequences of the act.[46]

Müller's joint effect of free will and necessity is in Whitney's case the joint effect of consciousness and unconsciousness. We will have to come back to this aspect, too.

How is it possible that two scholars of the highest rank could broadly agree in their views on the nature and development of language and nevertheless come to different conclusions – one claiming that language is a natural phenomenon, and the other that it is made by people?

3.3 IS LANGUAGE MADE BY PEOPLE?

Let us advance to the present. In his book *Rules and Representations*, Noam Chomsky tries to answer the question of whether languages are 'made by men' and whether they are, therefore, 'accessible to an approach quite different from that of the natural sciences'.[47] I do not want to attack Chomsky's basic argument because, in my view, he is right to say that the answer to this question is irrelevant to his topic. He intends to identify those mental structures which represent the ability of an idealised speaker to have the grammar of a language at his or her disposal. Of central importance to him is that core part of grammar which we as human beings have at our disposal from birth and which is thus (in principle) common to all languages. In this context it is irrelevant that a language is used by a speaker for the purpose of communication. Chomsky's problem is truly an empirical and scientific one, but on the condition that the following premiss is correct: 'that grammar has to have a real existence, that is, there is something in your brain that corresponds to the grammar'.[48]

I therefore do not want to hold it against him that he thinks the question of whether languages are 'made by man' is irrelevant. What is rather remarkable, however, is that he does not consider himself able meaningfully to interpret or pose this question at all. Let us have a closer look at one passage of his writing. In the course of a commentary on the thesis that we have 'made' our language, he writes that this claim is

> at best quite misleadingly formulated. Have we, as individuals, 'made' our language? That is, have you or I 'made' English? That seems either senseless or wrong. We had no choice at all as to the language we acquired; it simply developed in our minds by virtue of our internal constitution and environment. Was the language 'made' by our remote ancestors? It is difficult to make any sense of such a view. In fact, there is no more reason to think of language as 'made' than there is to think of the human visual system and the various forms that it assumes as 'made by us'.[49]

Chomsky confuses two problems that should be held apart. Have I created my own language? No, certainly not. My linguistic competence evolved during the first years of my life without my being able to do anything for or against it; indeed, it evolved as a result of my 'internal make-up and the environment'. If we interpret the thesis that English (for example) was man-made as meaning that the individual competence of the speakers of English was created by themselves, this is probably 'nonsensical or wrong'. But who would ever have claimed such nonsense? However, the question as to how human beings (children) come to have their mother tongue, which is Chomsky's central problem, is completely different from the question as to how the state of what one nowadays calls the 'English language' came about. The answer to the first question is largely independent of the answer to the second.

'Was language "made" by our remote ancestors?'

It is Chomsky's peculiar conception of language which makes it impossible for him to accept this question as meaningful. Chomsky thinks that what we commonly call 'a language', for example 'the English language', is an abstract phantasm which, first, has no real existence and which is, second, of no interest to the linguist at all. Real and interesting is exclusively the individual competence which is 'represented' in the brain of a speaker, or what Chomsky has recently called I-Grammar (internalised grammar). It is, indeed, impossible to ask meaningfully whether the representation in my head was made by people or not. But in the process, Chomsky overlooks that there is a relationship of mutual influence between the competence in my head and 'the German language' in the hypostatised sense, in the sense of effective conventions; and that, patholinguistic questions aside, the competence in my head is only of linguistic interest in so far as it agrees with the conventions. I shall come back to this topic in detail in section 5.3.

Returning to the initial questions posed at the end of the last section, how is it possible that given largely similar views about language, one person comes to the conclusion that it is man-made, whereas the other believes it to be a natural phenomenon?

The reason lies in the vagueness of the predicate 'man-made'. It is remarkably ambiguous.

An object (in the widest sense) can be man-made either because it is

A: the result of human actions,

or in the sense that it

B: came into existence as a result of human intentions.

Now, B implies A, but A does not imply B. This means that both criteria often apply simultaneously, but not necessarily. This relative independence was overlooked by the linguists of the nineteenth century. Those like Schleicher and Müller, who argued for the thesis that language is a natural phenomenon, denied that criterion B is applicable to a language: the development of a language (its 'growth') cannot be 'determined' by human beings; it is independent of the will of the individual.

Those who argued for the thesis that a language is a human institution and not a natural phenomenon, like Whitney, based their argument on A, 'that action is the only force that makes and changes language'.[50] These arguments do not, however, put the two parties in contradiction! Both are right, because the two positions are compatible. The supposed contradiction only came about because one party was forced to draw the inadmissible inference from non-B to non-A, and the other party was forced to draw the inadmissible inference from A to B. Differently expressed: since they tacitly assumed that A is equivalent to B, they were forced to accept the dichotomy $(-A \& -B)/(A \& B)$. Everything which is not natural has to be artificial.[51]

From the fact that B implies A, but A does not imply B, it follows that the 'classical' dichotomy has to be replaced by a trichotomy, because $B \supset A$ is equivalent to $-(-A \& B)$. Hence three possibilities remain: $(-A \& -B)/(A \& B)/(A \& -B)$. In other words,

1 There are things that are not the goal of human intentions and that are (therefore also) not the results of human actions (upright walk, the language of the bees, the weather, the Alps).
2 There are things which are the results of human actions and the goal of their intentions (Westminster Abbey, a cake, Esperanto).
3 There are things which are the result of human actions but not the goal of their intentions (inflation, the makeshift path across the lawn, our language).

Things of the first kind are undoubtedly natural phenomena; those of the second are undoubtedly artefacts.

The things of the third kind share a criterion with each of the others. They are, like those of the second kind, the results of human actions and they are, like those of the first kind, not the goal of human intentions. Hence they could be lumped with either the artefacts or the natural phenomena, depending on which criterion was given more importance.

I call those things which are the results of human action, but not the goal of their intentions, 'phenomena of the third kind'. The replacement of the classical dichotomical division of scientific explananda by this trichotomy can be illustrated graphically:

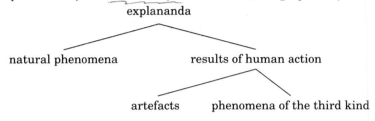

explananda

natural phenomena   results of human action

artefacts   phenomena of the third kind

As one can see, phenomena of the third kind are those Fergusonian 'establishments, which are indeed the results of human action, but not the execution of any human design'.[52]

First, I want to claim that natural languages are phenomena of the third kind, neither natural phenomena nor artefacts. Second, I would like to claim that regarding language as a phenomenon of the third kind achieves just what the linguists of the nineteenth century wanted to achieve, something which has stayed a desideratum up to the present day: the establishment of a conception of language which does justice to the eternal change in language.

Part II

Solution and discussion

Chapter 4

The working of the invisible hand

4.1 LANGUAGE – A PHENOMENON OF THE THIRD KIND

Summarising the substance of the last two chapters once again, there exists a fundamental error which makes it impossible for those who succumb to it to grasp the nature of human culture in general and that of language in particular. This error takes the following form: the world can be divided exclusively into two kinds of phenomena, those which are made by God (i.e., existing by nature), and those which are made by people. *Tertium non datur.* The works of God are natural phenomena; those of humans are artefacts. Natural phenomena exist independently of human will and are therefore the object of the natural sciences; artefacts are the products of voluntary actions and thus the object of the arts and cultural sciences. This fundamental error leads to a misinterpretation of language and linguistics. Those who want to count linguistics among the natural sciences can refer to the fact that language evolves independently of human will. Those who want to count linguistics among the arts and humanities can refer to the fact that only the linguistic acts of human beings could bring about the evolution of language.

The solution to this dilemma lies in the recognition that the assumed dichotomy 'natural phenomenon vs artefact' is based on an unidentified ambiguity inherent in the predicate 'man-made'. In other words, there exists yet a third kind of phenomena apart from natural phenomena and artefacts, and language is one of these phenomena.

I have already pointed out in section 1.2 that our ordinary language often prevents us from appropriately representing evolutionary processes. In this case we are faced with the same problem. It is noteworthy that we have the adjectives *natural* and *artificial*, but none to designate a phenomenon of the third kind. The reason for this discrepancy is probably that the latter are evolutionary phenomena (in a sense which remains to be explained). On the other hand, we clearly distinguish between the two ways in which something can be made by people. But we do it with completely inadequate terminology. Just as we distinguish correctly between natural flowers and artificial ones, we distinguish between natural forms of payment (money) and artificial forms of payment (substitutes for money), between a town that has grown naturally and an artificial town (planned on the drawingboard), between a natural alphabet and an artificial one, and finally between natural and artificial languages.

The distinctions themselves are correct, but the names we give them are misleading. 'Natural' forms of payment, towns, and alphabets have one fact in common: unlike natural flowers, they are not natural. They are human products and cultural institutions. What distinguishes them from their artificial counterparts, which are also human products and 'cultural phenomena'? We usually give the following answer to this question: while the latter are *planned*, the former have *grown organically*. The prison of fossilised expressions described in section 3.2 rears its ugly head again.

In everyday language we basically make the tripartite distinction introduced in the last chapter, but we make it with dichotomic terminology. With regard to things that are non-natural, we distinguish between 'natural' and 'artificial' ones, the 'natural' among them being our phenomena of the third kind. We represent this trichotomy in a form that can be illustrated as follows:

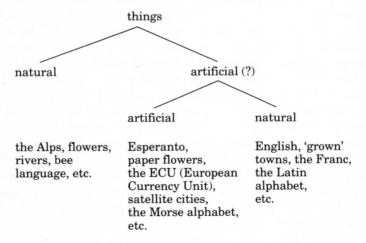

This diagram shows that we ordinarily use the adjective 'natural' ambiguously. The reason for calling phenomena of the third kind 'natural' as well probably lies in the fact that they indeed have features of natural phenomena, besides having features of artefacts. 'The things in this category', writes Haakonssen,[1] 'resemble natural phenomena in that they are unintended and have to be explained in terms of efficient causes, and they resemble artificial phenomena in that they are the result of human action.'

The essential properties of phenomena of the third kind can be more clearly demonstrated by providing an example.

Researchers in the field of road transport call a certain phenomenon which happens daily on our motorways the *traffic jam out of nowhere*. It is a phenomenon of the third kind which can be used to demonstrate the typical properties of this species. I would like to describe the genesis of such a traffic jam with the help of a simplified model.

Let us assume that cars are travelling at 100 km/h at a distance of about 30 metres from each other on a heavily used road (which is, for simplicity's sake, single-lane). One driver brakes suddenly (for reasons which are irrelevant here), reducing his speed to 90 km/h. We shall call this car or driver 'a' and the following ones 'b', 'c', etc. Seeing a's brakelights, b will brake too; as b does not know how much a has reduced his speed, b will brake too much rather than too little, so as to leave a safety margin. She will perhaps reduce her speed from 100 to 85 km/h. Driver c has a similar problem: reducing speed to exactly 85 km/h is too risky, as he does not know how hard b is braking. Trying to be safe, he will brake more than necessary, reducing his speed to perhaps 80 km/h. We can figure it out from here: s comes to a standstill, and along with all the cars that follow.

This is a simplified model. Reality is much more dramatic, as the speed would not be reduced linearly from car to car. But for our purposes this example will do.

The traffic jam from vehicle s onwards has in some way been 'made' by the drivers of the vehicles a to s. They have produced it through their actions, without each individual having the intention of doing so. Each one of them has only reacted appropriately to the actions of the one in front and with his or her own legitimate need for safety in mind, and so, without intending it or even knowing it, created a highly dangerous situation. (By the way, the curious thing about this type of traffic jam is that those who caused or 'made' it do not have to put up with it!)

As a rule, phenomena of the third kind such as this traffic jam are collective phenomena. They come into existence through the actions of many, and this because the actions generating the phenomenon are characterised by certain similarities, which may be irrelevant as such, but which together can have certain consequences. In our example the similarity lies in the fact that each of the drivers acts according to the maxim 'better brake a bit too much rather than a bit too little'. Each individual's intentions are directed towards not bumping into the car in front; in general, the drivers will not be aware of their contribution to a 'traffic jam out of nowhere'. The jam is thus an epiphenomenon of these actions of braking with a safety margin.

To express this situation in the language of action theory, one must widen the scope of its terminology.

In the theory of individual actions one normally distinguishes between the *result* of an action and its *consequences*.[2]

The *result* of an action 'a' is an event which has to happen for the action to be considered as having been executed at all. If the result of 'a' has occurred, one says of the action 'a' that it has been accomplished. The action of closing the door has thus been accomplished if the result, namely that the door is closed, has been achieved. (Whatever someone might have done, the action of closing the door does not count as executed if the door is not closed in the end.) I call the intention of bringing about the result of an action the *primary intention*.[3]

However, actions are normally not executed for the sake of their results, but for the sake of their consequences.

The intended effects of the results of an action 'a' are called the (intended) *consequences* of this action. Should the intended consequences of an action fail to occur, the action is said to be *unsuccessful*. Hence, an action can have been accomplished without being successful. (If I close the door to make the room warmer, it is still possible that the intended effect, the warming of the room, does not occur.) I call the intention of bringing about the consequence(s) of an action the *secondary intention*. According to this terminological rule, the traffic jam is neither the result nor the consequence of the actions that generated it. We are dealing instead with a kind of non-intended consequence. But this way of putting it is misleading, too, because the traffic jam is *not* a non-intended consequence of the individual actions. The traffic jam is the non-intended consequence of all the actions concerned taken together. There are numerous examples of non-intended consequences of individual actions here, most of which are uninteresting: a thermos tips over, or a briefcase slips from the seat. The consequence which is relevant to the emergence of the jam is certainly not non-intended. A reduction in speed – in this case rather too much than too little – is quite obviously intended. However, this generates the non-intended phenomenon. What is peculiar about these non-intended consequences, which represent phenomena of the third kind, is that you can bet your bottom dollar that they will occur, provided the actions producing them are accomplished.

In fact, we are dealing here with *causal* consequences of the actions' results. If the actions of the drivers a to s succeed in sufficiently reducing the speed of their own cars in relation to that of the one in front, including a safety margin, then the *consequence* is a standstill. It is sometimes claimed that it is wrong to assume causalities in the cultural sciences and the sciences of action.[4] This is quite obviously false. It is correct to say that cultural phenomena cannot be explained *exclusively* by reference to causality, but an explanation in the domain of cultural sciences can certainly have causal parts. To be adequate, our explanation of a phenomenon of the third kind must, in fact, have such a part. The reason for this is that phenomena of the third kind are always composed of a micro-domain which is intentional and a macro-domain which is causal by nature. The micro-domain is constituted by the individuals or their actions involved in the generation of the phenomenon; in our case these are the braking drivers. The macro-domain is the structure generated by the micro-domain; in our case, the 'traffic jam out of nowhere'. We can thus summarise that *a phenomenon of the third kind is the causal consequence of a multitude of intentional actions which serve, at least partially, similar intentions.* Neither Müller nor Whitney remained blind to the fact that factors such as these play a role in the process of growth or change in language (see section 3.2): Müller recognised that this process 'combines in one the two opposite elements of necessity and free will',[5] whereas Whitney noted that the process of 'language-making . . . works both consciously and unconsciously, as regards the further consequences of the act'.[6]

However, a contemporary of Müller and Whitney saw the attributes of those phenomena (our phenomena of the third kind) much more clearly. This man was, again, not a linguist, but a national economist: Carl Menger. In his work *Problems of Economics and Sociology*, which appeared in 1883 (and was translated in to English in 1963), he devoted a whole chapter to these phenomena. The second chapter of the third book bears the title 'The Theoretical Understanding of those Social Phenomena which are not a Product of Agreement or of Positive Legislation, but are Unintended Results of Historical Development'. He describes the following questions as 'perhaps the most noteworthy problem of social sciences', and continues, 'How can it be that institutions which serve the common welfare and are extremely significant for its development come into being without a common will directed towards establishing them?'[7]

'What is the nature of all the above social phenomena [namely, "Language, religion, law, even the state itself . . ., the phenomena of markets, of competition, of money"[8]] – this is the question of importance for our science – and how can we arrive at a full understanding of their nature and their movement?'[9]

In broad agreement with the conception of language as a phenomenon of the third kind, he writes: 'Law, language, the state, money, markets, all these social structures in their various empirical forms and in their constant change are to no small extent the unintended result of social development.'[10]

He vehemently rejects two types of pseudo-explanation:

'pragmatic understanding' and
organismic metaphors.

'The most obvious idea for arriving at understanding of social institutions, of their nature, and of their movement was to explain them as the result of human calculation aimed at their establishment and formation.'[11]

In Menger's view, this is 'pragmatic understanding'. Although this 'explanation' has, according to Menger, 'the advantage of interpreting from a common, easily understood point of view all social institutions', it has the disadvantage of being 'not adequate to real conditions and was thoroughly unhistorical'.[12]

To the 'meaningless' attempts at explanation belong, according to Menger, 'above all the attempts of those who think they have solved the problem involved merely by designating as "organic" the developmental process we are discussing'.[13]

Menger's final definition of the domain of phenomena, which I have called the domain of phenomena of the third kind, reads as follows:

The social phenomena of 'organic' origin . . . are characterised
by the fact that they present themselves to us as the unintended
result of individual efforts of members of society, i.e., of efforts in
pursuit of individual interests. Accordingly, in contrast to the
previously characterised social structures, they are . . . the unintended social result of individually teleological factors.[14]

In his writings, Carl Menger thus anticipated the theory of
phenomena of the third kind in its essential parts. An adequate
mode of explanation for these phenomena remains unclear in this
treatise. We are only told that the explanation has to be found 'in a
specifically sociological way', in the framework of *theoretical* 'social
research'.[15] The next chapter will be devoted to the mode of
explanation which I regard as adequate.

4.2 INVISIBLE-HAND EXPLANATIONS

It is said that everyone in the Balkans eats garlic; the explanation for
this – so I have heard – is that someone once started to eat garlic
inadvertently, and the others knew that the unpleasant odour was
unnoticeable as soon as one ate garlic oneself.

One way of ruining an interesting story is to analyse it. I would
like to do it nevertheless. What makes the above explanation
interesting? It obviously lies in its surprising twist. The explanation,
however implausible, is logically possible. The most obvious explanation, that everybody eats garlic because everybody likes the taste of
it, is replaced by the rather droll thesis that everybody eats garlic
because nobody can stand the smell of it. It is indeed the case that
if every single person counters the disagreeable situation of being
exposed to the smell of garlic by eating garlic, the end effect will be
that everybody will eat garlic regularly, if only one member of the
community has started to do so for whatever reason. Provided that
the premises are true, this result must follow.

In terms of the theoretical framework sketched here, this story
about the general habit of eating garlic is a *phenomenon of the third
kind*; the fact that everybody eats garlic because nobody can stand
the smell of it is one of *Mandeville's paradoxes*, and the explanation
for their general habit is an *invisible-hand explanation*.

I would now like to explain more fully the form of an invisible-
hand explanation, or, as I will also call it, an invisible-hand theory.
But first to the name itself.

The choice of this name has advantages and disadvantages. It is a disadvantage that the metaphor of the invisible hand can mislead those unfamiliar with the term, seemingly referring to something mysterious and obscure. However, the opposite is true. An invisible-hand theory attempts to explain structures and reveal processes, namely those structures which are produced by human beings who do not intend or even notice them, as if they were 'led by an invisible hand'.[16] The metaphor of the invisible hand was created by Adam Smith, who used it in the famous passage already quoted (in section 2.3), and even earlier in other works.[17] The disadvantage of this metaphor (that it is rather misleading for the layperson) is compensated for by the fact that it is generally known and established in the domain of political philosophy and economic theory.

The expression 'invisible-hand explanation' itself seems to have been coined by Robert Nozick:

> There is a certain lovely quality to explanations of this sort. They show how some overall pattern or design, which one would have thought had to be produced by an individual's or group's successful attempt to realize the pattern, instead was produced and maintained by a process that in no way had the overall pattern or design 'in mind'. After Adam Smith, we shall call such explanations *invisible-hand explanations*.[18]

Generally speaking, we can say, again with Robert Nozick, that 'an invisible-hand explanation explains what looks to be the product of someone's intentional design, as not being brought about by anyone's intentions.'[19] It is a kind of genetic explanation.[20] It explains a phenomenon, its explanandum, by explaining how it came into existence or could have come into existence. It is especially useful in the explanation of social institutions such as money, language, taste, ghettos, etc.; that is to say, socio-cultural structures which might easily give rise to the idea (and quite often did so) that they were created intentionally by a central planning instance, an inventor, god, or central committee.

All these institutions, which are, of course, without exception, phenomena of the third kind, can be perceived and described on a micro-level as well as on a macro-level, as we have already seen in the previous chapter. But perceiving them on one level does not necessarily mean perceiving them on the other. We often find it trendy to choose the more expensive of two similar products, regretting the rate of inflation at the same time. We can deplore the change in our language as decay without seeing a connection to our own habits of speech. 'Young people really don't know their grammar any more, because nowadays they don't learn it in school.' In short, the consideration of the macro-level of a social institution is in principle independent of the consideration of the micro-level of the individual actions that produce it. This is true not only of ordinary life, but also of scientific considerations. We can draw a map of Manhattan which represents the different residential areas of the various ethnic groups there, without ever asking the question as to how this ethnic segregation actually came about. We can even draw diachronic maps which show, for example, how long Harlem was a Jewish quarter and from what time onwards blacks settled in it, without any reference to the movement of the inhabitants and their motives. Such a procedure is very much the rule in linguistics. Histories of a language generally state that certain words 'displaced others' or 'replaced' them; that they 'spread', 'advance', 'penetrate', and whatever other hypostatising metaphors may be found.[21] Very seldom is a link established with the language behaviour of the speaking individuals who produce these 'spreads', 'advances', and 'replacements'. That is to say, one either forgoes any attempt at explanation and is satisfied with describing the facts or mistakenly believes the description to be the explanation.[22]

An *explanation* of such a two-level social institution only can consist in deducing the second level, the macro-level of the institution, from the first level, the micro-level of individual social actions. This is exactly what an invisible-hand theory wants to achieve. Edna Ullmann-Margalit characterises this as follows:

> An invisible-hand explanation explains a well-structured social pattern or institution. It typically replaces an easily forthcoming and initially plausible explanation according to which the explanandum phenomenon is the product of intentional design with a rival account according to which it is brought about through a process involving the separate actions of many individuals who are supposed to be minding their own business unaware of and *a fortiori* not intending to produce the ultimate overall outcome.[23]

'Its true definition', wrote Wilhelm von Humboldt in reference to language, 'can . . . only be a genetic one.' This is actually true for all phenomena of the third kind. Harlem is a black ghetto; so is

Soweto. But the two are essentially different phenomena. Whereas the former has 'grown organically' and is therefore a phenomenon of the third kind,[24] the latter is the artefact of racists.[25]

To understand a phenomenon of the third kind one must know its process of formation as well as the result of this process, because a phenomenon of the third kind is not only one of the two, process of formation or result; it is both. What we simply call results – New High German, modern morals, the buying power of the dollar, the ghetto of Harlem – are not end-results of processes of formation, but episodes in processes of cultural evolution whose beginning and end cannot be specified.

An invisible-hand explanation reflects the three essential attributes of phenomena of the third kind:

(i)   they are procedural by nature;
(ii) they are constituted by a micro-level and a macro-level;
(iii) they have something in common with artefacts as well as with natural phenomena.

Ideally, an invisible-hand theory should contain three steps:

1 the depiction of the motives, intentions, goals, convictions (and such like) on which the actions of the individuals who participate in the generation of the phenomenon in question are based, including the general conditions of their actions;
2 the depiction of the process that explains the generation of structure by the multitude of individual actions;
3 the depiction of the structure generated by these actions.

A very simple example is the theory of the footpath or beaten path. The lawns of our universities are criss-crossed by networks of such paths. These networks have been 'laid out' in a very clever and economic way. Their structure is quite obviously more sensible than the structure of those paved paths planned by the architects. Furthermore, given a map representing the buildings and other institutions along with their functions, but no paths, one could easily anticipate where footpaths or beaten paths would emerge. A system of footpaths could be predicted with a far greater degree of accuracy than a system of the paved paths planned by architects. What is the reason for this? The system of footpaths has a more 'rational' structure; it is more 'intelligent' and, as a solution to traffic problems, much more elegant. However, it is obvious that far less intelligence went into the creation of the footpaths than into the design of the network of paved paths. The system of footpaths does not owe its 'intelligence' to the intelligence of its producers but to their laziness. My invisible-hand theory of this system is therefore the following: I hypothesise that most people resemble each other in preferring to take a shorter rather than a longer route. I observe that the paved paths do not correspond to this tendency, as they often do not represent the shortest connection between those points most often frequented by people at a university. I know that a lawn withers in those places that are most often trodden on. I therefore assume that the system of footpaths is the non-intended causal consequence of all those (intentional, finalistic) actions which consist in reaching certain goals by foot under the maxim of saving energy.

This theory incorporates the three levels of the ideal model: the generating maxims of action have been enumerated (choosing a route acording to the maxim of energy-saving); the invisible-hand process is identified as the gradual destruction of the lawn on this route; the third level is represented by the fixed structure which emerges over time, its description of which I have omitted here.

This theory also accommodates, as requested, the three essential attributes of a phenomenon of the third kind: its procedural character, the division into a micro-level and a macro-level, and the fact that it has features of an artefact as well as features of a natural phenomenon. The theory is in part finalistic in its explanation, typical of explanations of artefacts, but it also contains a causal explanatory part which normally characterises explanations of natural phenomena.

An invisible-hand explanation explains its explanandum, a phenomenon of the third kind, as the causal consequence of individual intentional actions which are based on at least partially similar intentions.

Although I have never empirically observed the emergence of a footpath, I think that this theory is basically correct (although it could be better formulated). Why this confidence? Could it not be as false as the garlic theory could be? What makes an invisible-hand explanation a good explanation?

Let us look at the triadic structure of an invisible-hand explanation again. It contains, like any other explanation

1 formulation of the premises and/or antecedent conditions,
2 general laws,
3 a depiction of the phenomenon to be explained.

Items 1 and 2 together form the explanans; 3 is the explanandum.

In the case of a phenomenon of the third kind, a process begins which is based on the antecedent conditions, the actions of individuals, and general laws; this process is the invisible-hand process, at the end of which we find the phenomenon that is to be explained.

Our theory of the footpaths contains two factors as premisses: on the one hand propositions about the ecology of actions (empirical propositions about conditions on the university campus: the buildings, their functions, etc.), including the description of traffic between the relevant points of the campus; on the other hand, propositions about the motives, habits, etc. of the individuals, assuming that people at the university tend to choose routes according to the degree of energy they can save.

The general laws can be of a logical–mathematical or a causal nature. The explanation of the footpath uses a general law of causality, which says that a lawn withers or dies in those places that are frequently walked over. The garlic theory uses a logical–mathematical law: if almost all contacts of those who eat garlic eat garlic themselves, the eating of garlic spreads epidemically.

In both cases the explanandum occurs necessarily provided that the premisses are true. Our initial question was 'Under which circumstances is an invisible-hand explanation a good explanation?'

It is good first and foremost if it is true; it is true if the premisses are true, if the general laws are valid, and if the invisible-hand process leads necessarily to the explanandum.

However, the truth value of an invisible-hand theory cannot be established in most cases, as the truth of the essential premisses cannot be ascertained. In many cases the truth value of propositions about the motives of actions cannot be verified or falsified, due to either technical or psychological reasons. Furthermore, the invisible-hand phenomenon is often concealed from observation. An invisible-hand explanation is usually a conjectural story.

However, this does not necessarily diminish the explanatory value of an invisible-hand explanation. It can be **good** or **bad**, independent of our ability to check its truth value. It is good if the premisses are **plausible** and if the invisible-hand process is **cogent**. Plausibility and cogency are the criteria of adequacy for an invisible-hand theory.

The garlic theory was cogent. This constitutes its value as a baffling anecdote. But its premiss is not plausible. If I could not stand the smell of garlic, I would rather avoid garlic-eaters than eat garlic myself, as I would not like the smell of garlic on myself either; and above all, I would like to avoid annoying others with a smell which they dislike as much as I do. In contrast, the strength of the footpath theory lies in the plausibility of the assumption that, on the whole, people tend to use shorter rather than longer routes, and the inexorability with which – should this premiss be true – footpaths emerge under these circumstances.

Let us assume that there is a large lawn between the entrance to the university library and the entrance to the university restaurant; the paved pathways lead around the lawn at right angles. This is the ideal condition for the emergence of a footpath.

Is it possible to predict that a footpath will actually emerge? If the situation described above existed anywhere in Germany right now, I would bet on it, but I would not bet my last penny. What conclusion would we arrive at, however, if we were to imagine this situation in North Korea, 200 years ago in Berlin, or 200 years from now around here? I would not risk a bet, because I lack the knowledge that would enable me to anticipate how people would act. Are there bans on walking on lawns? To what extent are these bans enforced? How disciplined are the people concerned? What is their attitude towards infringements of rules? What is their attitude towards lawns?

I would not even dare to make a long-term prediction about my own behaviour. At present, I am willing to take a shortcut over a lawn, for example, but not across a flowerbed or a lawn covered with crocuses. Will my willingness to walk across the lawn be more or less in twenty-five years? Both could be possible. Perhaps I will have extended my present protectiveness towards flowers to the lawn itself.

This shows that invisible-hand explanations have only a very restricted prognostic value. If anything, they are all predictions of a hypothetical nature: 'If people act according to this or that maxim, such-and-such a structure will emerge, under such-and-such general conditions.' We are acquainted with this type of 'prediction' in economics, and we know how unreliable it is.

As far as phenomena of the third kind (which are more complex than a system of footpaths) are concerned, it is impossible to make any specific prediction. At most, general ones can be made – so-called 'pattern predictions'. The law of gravity allows us to make predictions about the behaviour of an apple. So-called market laws, however, do not allow us to make predictions about the job situation of unemployed Mr Smith, but rather at most about the development of unemployment in general. One can venture to forecast that the unstressed syllables in German will continue to disappear but it cannot be predicted that *haben* will have become *ham* in a few hundred years. It can only be guessed at.

Invisible-hand theories do not have a prognostic value in the sense in which physical theories have a prognostic value, and this is because of the impossibility of predicting the premises. They enable us, however, to make trend extrapolations: 'If this or that is the case, people will behave in this or that way, and then such-and-such structures will emerge.'

National economists might deplore the lack of prognostic value of their invisible-hand theories, but this is not such a grave problem for linguists, for the following reasons: first, it is an error to assume in the domain of the arts and social sciences that the 'scientificity' of a theory is directly related to its prognostic value, and second, there is much less practical need for linguistic predictions.

An invisible-hand theory is first and foremost of *diagnostic* value. Casually put, it explains not how things will develop in the future, but how they came to be the way they are.

But what is the value of a diagnosis, one might ask, if not to give an orientation for the future? The point of a medical diagnosis, for example, is to be the basis for therapy. Diagnoses are not produced for their own sake.

In order to judge the value of a diagnostic theory of language, we have to remember what was said in section 1.4. Nature, change, and genesis correspond closely to each other in phenomena of the third kind. It is not our task to predict the structure of the English of the future, but to contribute to an *understanding of what we do when we communicate*. When we understand the maxims and rules of communication, we will also understand why our language has changed in the course of time and why it will continue to change. The changes of tomorrow are the collective consequences of our communicative actions today. We have to discover those maxims, motives, and rules of our communicative actions which prompt the invisible-hand process and at the end of which stand the structures to be explained.

In spite of their restricted predictive value, (good) invisible-hand explanations are explanations in the strict sense of the word. Roger Lass, for example, in his book *On Explaining Language Change*, advocates the view that there are no explanations for language change because there are no laws in the domain of language.[26] For this reason, too, language change cannot be predicted. Truth is mixed with falsehood here. It is true that there are no laws governing human actions, such as that under certain conditions people will avoid one of two homonyms or walk diagonally over the lawn. It is also true, for this reason, that the disappearance of a certain homonym or the emergence of a certain footpath cannot be predicted. It is false that there are no possible explanations (in the strict sense) for these phenomena. Laws are simply sought and demanded in the wrong place. The actions of people are based on the antecedent conditions, and there are no laws that predict whether they will occur or not. Laws allow us to predict only *if* the antecedent conditions are fulfilled. If the speakers of a language stop using a certain word, it disappears from the language; if we step frequently on the same place on a lawn, the lawn withers there. The correct impression of the banality of these predictions lies in the strength of the laws they are based on!

Language change can be explained in principle on the basis of laws. It is unpredictable, however, not for lack of laws, but because it cannot be predicted whether the premisses will be fulfilled. In most cases we only observe *post festum*, on the basis of the explanandum's existence, that the premisses *were* fulfilled. That is to say, we know the explanandum, we know the laws, and we reconstruct the premisses. This is the point of diagnostic explanations. Trend extrapolations are not predictions based on uncertain laws, but predictions based on uncertain premisses.[27]

Invisible-hand explanations are often characterised by an element of surprise.[28] This may contribute to the fact that, as Nozick remarks, they 'have a certain lovely quality'.[29] But this means more than just an enhancement of their entertainment value. The element of surprise is also closely related to their explanatory power.

The real factor contributing to the explanatory power of a theory is not only its truth or cogency. Circular explanations are an example of true explanations without explanatory value. They are situated at one end of a continuum, and at the other extreme are invisible-hand explanations. The parameter according to which explanations are placed on the continuum of explanatory power is the 'distance' between the domain from which the explanatory concepts are taken and the domain of the explanandum. A circular explanation represents one extreme; the distance between the concepts of the explanans and the explanandum is zero. The concepts are identical. In the case of an invisible-hand explanation, this distance is typically very large. Whereas the central notions of the explanans belong mainly to the realm of psychology and sociology, the explanandum belongs mainly to the realm of legal and political philosophy, linguistics, economics, etc., or represents geometrical or other figures. We obviously find explanations more satisfying the less the concepts used have *prima facie* anything to do with the object to be explained. This discrepancy is often reinforced by the paradoxical Mandevillean form of the explanation (laziness/intelligent structure of the footpaths, individual egoism/prosperity for all, desire to be safe/traffic jam).

In his book *History of Biological Theories*, Rádl, a specialist in the philosophy of the Scottish Enlightenment, has called this mode of explanation the 'psychological–logical method'. He characterises it as follows: one usually starts with a 'psychological analysis of society' so as to extract one or two 'basic principles' and to establish them as the 'driving force'. One then proceeds to 'deduce' 'what would happen in a society' which followed these basic principles. 'Psychological–logical method' is thus a fitting label for this mode of explanation. The invisible-hand theory represents the generalisation of this method.[30]

Looking at an example from German, we see that expressions that refer to women in that language undergo a continual process of pejoration. This was the fate of the words *Weib* and *Frauenzimmer*, and the word *Frau* does not seem to be able to escape it either. How does this happen?

Representatives of linear thinking might suspect that there is a latent hostility towards women in our society underlying this trend, which motivates the individual speaker to use such a word 'a bit more pejoratively' every time. But how does one manage to use a word 'a bit more pejoratively'? Alma Graham postulates 'the tendency in the language that I called 'praise him/blame her'.[31] The pejoration of the expressions *Weib*, *Frau*, and others was, however, not so much the result of the maxim 'blame her', but more likely of the maxim 'praise her'. Here we encounter Mandeville's paradox again, according to which everyone is well-intentioned and nevertheless creates pejoration.

In a society like ours with a courtly tradition, there exists a rule of gallantry towards women. Men help women into their coats, offer them chairs, light their cigarettes, and so on. Part and parcel of this gallant behaviour is a tendency, when talking with or about women, to choose expressions that tend to belong to a higher level of style or social standing rather than a lower one. The maxim is therefore not 'blame her', but – to put it casually – 'in case of doubt choose an expression that is a notch too high rather than too low'. In the course of time, the 'next higher' word becomes the normal expression, whereas the formerly normal one is pejorised. This is why in restaurants these days the normal sign on the toilet is *Damen* (ladies), whereas *Frauen* (women) belongs more to the style used in public amenities. The expression *Wie geht es Ihrer Frau?* (How is your wife?) is regarded in some situations as unbecoming; one should say *Frau Gemahlin* or *Gattin* (spouse).

It goes without saying that the aforementioned maxim is only valid if the gallantry game is actually played. Where it is not played, it can be rather embarrassing to refer to women as *Damen*. In the sentence *those men and women who have become innocent victims of the robbery ...*, the substitution of *ladies and gentlemen* for *men and women* would be inappropriate. That is to say, the choice of words in this lexical field has nothing to do with a high or low opinion, with common politeness or with the social status of the persons in question, but depends on whether or not it is appropriate to play the game of gallantry. This is why tennis clubs have *Damenabteilungen* (ladies' sections), but hospitals have *Frauenabteilungen* (women's wards), in which one can find *Damentoiletten* (ladies' toilets). *Damenrechtlerin* (fighter for ladies' rights) sounds as curious as *Frauenwahl* (women's choice) at a dance.

To summarise, the individual's wish to be gallant leads in the long run, on the level of language, to pejoration, as if guided by an invisible hand. We are dealing here with a form of inflation.[32]

This example provides yet another opportunity to ask whether an invisible-hand explanation is useful or not. Provided my explanation of this type of pejoration is a good one, what does it achieve and what does it fail to achieve? It cannot be used to make predictions about the semantic development of the words *Frau* or *Dame*. It allows us, however, to make the structural prediction that pejoration will continue if the rules of gallantry continue to be practised. Whether the game of gallantry will continue to be played in the future depends on many social factors, my opinion of which I will refrain from expressing.

However, I believe that the explanation has some diagnostic value. This value increases with the degree to which the explanation is made more detailed and subtle by linguistic and historical investigations. It gives us insight into one aspect of our speech, its functions and macro-structural effects.

As 'theorists, we know nothing of human *language* unless we understand human *speech*',[33] writes Peter Strawson, exaggerating somewhat. But it would not be an exaggeration unless it were basically true.

4.3 CAUSAL, FINAL, AND FUNCTIONAL EXPLANATIONS

Comparing the process of the production of linguistic phenomena with that of a footpath is nothing new. In 1912, Fritz Mauthner had already used this comparison in the same way.

> If all the farmers of a village believe they have found the shortest way to the next church or pub, by crossing a certain meadow, for example, . . . a path on which no grass grows will be stamped out quite mechanically. . . . It is then quite appropriate figuratively to call this a natural law. . . . However, . . . there is of course no active natural law which drives the village to the shortest route . . .; there is no village, only farmers; . . . there is only the firmly trampled clay on the one hand, and the steps of the walking farmers on the other . . .. But every time the highly individual farmer momentarily lifts his individual leg to take a step in a certain direction, there is also a psychological factor, which one can call will or habit, depending on the circumstances. . . . Just the same is true for those movements of man which are summarised under the name of language.[34]

Mauthner wrote this with regard to the neogrammarian thesis that phonetic laws are valid without exception. He had obviously realised quite clearly how final and causal factors interact. This interaction of two factors in the process of language change or its equal, the development of a language's condition, was already known in the late nineteenth century, as we have seen. Max Müller wrote that 'The process through which language is settled and unsettled combines in one the two opposite elements of necessity and free will';[35] and William D. Whitney wrote somewhat later that 'The process of language-making . . . works both consciously and unconsciously, as regards the further consequences of the act.'[36]

In spite of this correct and decisive insight, these two linguists were unsuccessful in using it to create a consistent concept of language that implied the idea of evolution. The interaction of two 'opposing' factors seems indeed to be a general characteristic of evolutionary processes. The interaction of the two factors 'free will and necessity', observed by Max Müller in language evolution, corresponds to the interaction of the factors 'chance and necessity' in the evolution of animate nature.

Oddly, Müller and Whitney's approach was never pursued, but unfortunately forgotten, at least in the domain of linguistics. Rather than considering this interaction, one concentrated again on the old cul-de-sac, that is, on the question of whether language evolution is a final or a causal process. 'Time changes all things; there is no reason why language should escape this universal law', wrote Saussure[37] with disarming simplicity in his *Cours*. Reversing the order of things, Armin Ayren says 'Language lives, and what lives, changes.'[38]

Among contemporary linguists, Eugenio Coseriu was the first of the authors known to me to level fundamental criticisms against, and decisively reject, the question concerning the causal reasons of language change. In his work *Synchrony, Diachrony and History*, which was published as early as 1958 in Spanish and can still be regarded as a fundamental work on the theory of language change, Coseriu wrote: 'The idea of a "causality" . . . is left over from the old conception of language as a "natural organism" and from the positivistic dream of discovering the putative "laws" of language (or of the languages) and of turning linguistics into an "exact science" in analogy with the natural sciences.'[39] As more recent work on grammatical theory has shown, this 'positivistic dream' has now become a rather integral part of reality. Those like Chomsky and his school, who are looking for genetically determined structures of human language, are working in the domain of human biology;[40] they may be justified in claiming that they use the procedures of the natural sciences, or the 'Galilean method', as it is sometimes called. But because the genetically determined part of our linguistic faculty, the only part which sets the limited framework for possible changes, remains untouched by the historical evolution of language (leaving aside the phylogenetic changes of our species), Coseriu is basically right in saying that causal theories are unsuitable to explain language change. However, in putting forward his own alternative, he shows that he, too, is still (or again) a prisoner of the natural–artificial dichotomy. 'In natural phenomena one must doubtlessly look for external necessity; in cultural phenomena, however, for inner necessity or finality.'[41] Coseriu's postulate of the thesis of finality is based on the right premisses: that language is 'not a natural object . . . but a cultural object',[42] that it is 'a world . . . created by man'.[43] It is also based, however, on the false, dogmatic assumption that cultural objects created by people should necessarily be explained in a finalistic way, 'because free human activities are always motivated by their *what for* and not by their causal *why*.'[44]

Just like the nineteenth-century authors who became entangled in the natural–artificial dichotomy, Coseriu's writing is marked by a certain uneasiness, an effort to find a way out. It is clear that he, too, knows that the speakers of a language generally do not intend to produce change in their language, and that they are generally not aware of language change taking place. He is therefore correct in saying that Henri Frei's concept of 'finalité inconsciente', un-conscious finality, is obscure, although he is unable to clarify the issue. 'The only fact which is true . . . is, that – except for special cases . . . – finality emerges spontaneously and immediately when there is a need for expression, not as a reflected intention to change the interindividual language.'[45]

How, then, can we continue meaningfully to discuss finality?

As we have seen, finality plays a role in language change, but in connection with causal processes.

The results of final, or as I prefer to say, intentional[46] actions accumulate under certain conditions and bring about structures which do not lie within the sphere of final individual actions. The accumulation is a causal phenomenon. Thus, both the 'finalists' and the 'causalists' have a share of the truth. Their error lies in the exclusivity of their claims, as both fail to notice the interaction of final and causal processes. Their one-sided way of looking at things may be the cause of this error. For those who regard a linguistic change from the perspective of the linguistic phenomenon per-ceive nothing but causality. This is indeed the case: the fact that people have changed their preference of expression – for whatever reason – has caused the German *englisch* in the meaning of 'angelic', for example, to disappear from the German language. The discontinuation of an expression's use interrupts the trans-mission chain in the form of a teaching–learning relay, which causes (in the strictly causal sense) the 'disappearance' of this expression from the language.

By contrast, those who regard a linguistic change from the

perspective of the communicating people will discover only finality. Admittedly, they will (in general) not find finality directed towards change, but towards the success of each individual communicative goal. At a certain point in time, anyone speaking of the *englische Mädchen* (the angelic or the English maiden), intending to refer to an angelic figure, ran the communicative risk of being misunderstood. A decision not to use the word *englisch* (in this sense) was therefore not **caused** – for example by homonymy – but **based** on the wish not to be misunderstood. The homonymy does not represent the cause of a change, but as Coseriu correctly observes, a **condition** under which speakers generally tend to choose an alternative for one of the homonymous expressions in situations in which they believe they might otherwise be misunderstood. But this does not make the **change of a language** a finalistic phenomenon, because the change is not intended. Only the choice of an alternative expression in a context that could provoke misunderstanding is final. The resulting change is its causal consequence.

Let us have a look at the following two types of statements which one can find in any history of language:

1 The cause for the disappearance of *englisch₁* (angelic) from the German language was its homonymy with *englisch₂* (English).
2 *Englisch₁* has disappeared from German because it was homonymous with *englisch₂*.

Are those statements wrong? Are they without explanatory power? They are not completely wrong, and they seem to have explanatory power. But on closer inspection, one recognises immediately that homonymy was neither necessary nor sufficient for the disappearance of *englisch₁*: could *englisch₁* not have disappeared without being homonymous with another word? Perhaps; perhaps not. We simply do not know. Did *englisch₁* necessarily have to disappear because of the homonymy? No, for there are enough homonyms in our language without causing any so-called homonym conflict, and secondly, *englisch₂* could have disappeared and been replaced by another word.

Why is it that some linguists so readily accept statements such as 1 or 2 as explanations? How can one possibly think that one is dealing with an explanation when two facts are presented, neither of which is a necessary or sufficient condition for the other to occur, let alone for both of them to occur? The reason is the abuse of the expressions 'cause' and 'because', which seem to give 1 and 2 the appearance of explanatory power. Let us consider the causes and reasons for the disappearance of *englisch*₁ one by one.

The word *englisch*₁ has not disappeared because it was homonymous with *englisch*₂, but **because**, at a certain time, it was no longer part of the vocabulary of the members of the speech community. It was no longer part of the vocabulary **because** it was no longer learned for this use. It was no longer learned **because** those who still knew the word avoided it and used alternative expressions such as *engelhaft* (angelic) instead. They avoided *englisch*₁ **because** they did not want to risk being misunderstood. This risk existed **because** *englisch*₁ was homonymous with *englisch*₂ and **because** the meanings of *englisch*₁ and *englisch*₂ were such that, in almost any sentence containing the word *englisch*₁ (angelic), this word could be replaced by *englisch*₂ without rendering that statement nonsensical (a choir of *englisch*₁ girls, an *englisch*₁ greeting, *englisch*₁ customs, *englisch*₁ miracles).[47]

The opposite was not true (an *englisch*₂ lawn, *englisch*₂ cloth, horse, etc.); that is to say, in most contexts, *englisch*₂ could not be replaced by *englisch*₁ without rendering the proposition nonsensical (or bizarre or improbable, etc.). **Because** this was not possible, the use of *englisch*₂ ran much less risk of being misinterpreted. ***Because*** for the homonymic pair, *englisch*₁ was more of a hazard to successful communication than *englisch*₂, *englisch*₂ was probably more frequently used. And **because** there was an easy alternative for *englisch*₁, based on the existence of the noun *Engel* and the possibilities afforded by German word formation, people tended to avoid *englisch*₁, using an alternative expression rather than *englisch*₂.

Statement 2 represents at best a very rough 'abbreviation' of all these explanatory steps forming a *because*-chain. (I suppose that, among other things, we tend to take such an abbreviation for an explanation because we usually regard the *because*-relation as transitive in ordinary language use.) However, if we unfold the 'abbreviation', it turns out to be a reconstruction of the route leading from the motives of acting individuals to the change that results from them in the macro-domain, thus turning into an invisible-hand explanation.

It is not always possible to reformulate the *because*-sentences of our explanation in such a way that they contain the word *cause*. This is why propositions 1 and 2 are not equivalent. The reason is that we use *because* for the representation of an (intentional) reason, as well as for the representation of a (causal) cause:

(1) I have written to you because I wanted to make you happy.
(2) I am wet because I fell into the water.

In sentence (1), *because* expresses a relation of justification ('A because B' means here 'B is the/a reason for A'), whereas sentence (2) expresses a relation of cause and effect ('A because B' means here 'B is the/a cause of A'). We could call the first *because* the intentional *because*, the second the causal *because*. The intentional *because* corresponds to *why* questions as well as *what for* questions; the causal *because* corresponds only to *why* questions. One could call the answers to *what for* questions finalistic explanations. But because each *what for* question can be expressed as an equivalent (intentional) *why* question, we need not distinguish the finalistic explanation (forward looking) from the corresponding one (backward looking), and we can quite generally talk about intentional explanations or questions.

The explanation gains precision if we reformulate it in sentences containing the words *cause* or *reason*, or if we introduce a distinction between the causal *because* and the intentional *because*. I have already done so tacitly: **bold-italic printing** represents the intentional *because*, **bold-only printing** represents the causal *because*. If you read our *because*-chain again in this new light, you will notice that the disappearance of *englisch*₁ was the causal consequence of individual intentional actions based on at least partially similar intentions.[48]

Strictly speaking, the explanation is still lacking. The time of the disappearance still remains to be explained. It seems to have happened by the middle of the last century. Why just then? Why not sooner or later? Is it possible that, with the advent of industrialisation, one suddenly talked more about England than about angels? Or was it suddenly fashionable to talk more frequently about angel-hood, so that a latent homonymic conflict became virulent? I would like to come back to this question in the next chapter.

It is sometimes said that invisible-hand explanations do not take social and historical facts into account. This criticism is as unjustified as saying that Darwinian evolutionary theory neglected the climate. The social and historical facts, as well as the linguistic facts, belong to those combined factors which motivate the speakers (or some speakers) of a language to modify their manner of speech or shift their preferences of expression. Those factors are, so to speak, the ecological conditions of action.

Invisible-hand explanations and historical explanations are not alternative forms of explanation, as is sometimes claimed; on the contrary, historical explanations represent (among other things) possible factors that influence the communicative actions of the speakers. However, the explanation must always be based on individual actions. There is no direct route from historical facts to linguistic facts which could claim to be an explanation.

We have seen that the explanation of the genesis of a linguistic fact cannot be solely formulated either on the intentional (finalistic) or on the causal level. Those who talk about 'the causes of language change' can claim by way of excuse that they did not use the word 'cause' in any precise way. What they meant were factors which would be the reasons for the communicative actions of speakers. But how can we explain the misconception that a theory of language should always be a finalistic one? I think there are two reasons for this error. First, there is the existence of the old dichotomic dogma: 'In natural phenomena one can doubtlessly find an external necessity or *causality*; in cultural phenomena, by contrast, one finds inner necessity or *finality*.'[49] Second, this error is based, I suppose, on the tacit assumption that a functionalist explanation is necessarily a finalistic one as well; in other words, that only a finalistic explanation can be functionalist.

What is more natural, indeed, than the supposition that cultural products which fulfil certain functions are *precisely made* to fulfil these functions? Linguistic phenomena often have a specific function. Hence, to explain their functionality, one must pose a finalistic question. Ronneberger-Sibold says this clearly and distinctly: 'In seeking the explanation of language change in the satisfaction of the needs of the language users, we become members of the group of "finalists" . . . whose question is "*what* do language users change their language *for*?"'[50]

In section 1.4 I indicated that questions concerning genesis and function are inextricably linked. To repeat: if we knew *what* we use our language *for*, we would also know *why* it changes all the time through our acts of communication. Thus, an invisible-hand explanation provides not only an explanation of the process of genesis, but is also a functionalist explanation. This deserves further comment.

If we ask the question about functionality with regard to social institutions or, more generally speaking, social systems, we must distinguish between two things: the system's function in the social life of the group in which the social institution is valid, and the functions of parts of the system in the system itself.

It seems indisputable that language has a function for us human beings. However, what this function is or originally was is somewhat less indisputable. A language helps in the exchange of thoughts, the transmission of acquired knowledge, the co-ordination of the hunt and similar things. 'The increasing co-operation in social communities, for example, in the use of tools and in hunting in groups required a differentiated mode of communication. Human language using words emerged as a new *medium of transport for the information flow*', writes Günther Osche.[51] To be useful in the co-ordination of hunting in groups, a language (and the intellect of the speaker) must have been already well advanced. In my story about Charlie,[52] I used the assumption that language was primarily an instrument used to influence fellow ape-men. This assumption has three advantages. It allows us to explain why it is an advantage for a single individual to master this instrument better than others (especially if the instrument plays a role in the choice of a partner). Second, one does not have to suppose a major jump between animal and human communication. Saltationist theories are always confronted with the problem of explaining the jump itself besides what they actually want to explain, the obstacle which caused Herder's failure. (Incidentally, if one holds the opinion that there were no jumps in evolution, but that it proceeded without interruptions, one is not necessarily obliged to suppose that it always proceeded at a steady speed.) Third, the supposition that the function of language in our life is primarily to influence others is in accord with the views of those contemporary philosophers of language who can be taken seriously, such as Herbert P. Grice.[53] The other functions listed above, which are doubtless part of our elaborate language (the transmission of thought, the co-ordination of the hunt, etc.) should not be denied or dismissed, but here we are dealing with functions derived from the function of influencing others. Why do I impart my thoughts to you? Obviously, to influence you; to reinforce your views or to modify them.

What does the term 'functionalist explanation' really mean? The function of a thing (a system, a part of a system) is its contribution to the functioning[54] of a superordinate system which it serves. The clock serves the human being, the hand of the clock serves the clock. A functionalist explanation of an object (in the most general sense) thus explains why it exists, why it still exists, or why it no longer exists. According to Edna Ullmann-Margalit, a description of function has the following general form:

The function of x in a system s is Φ

means

The system s has capacity/goal Ψ, and the Φ-ing of x is an essential element in the explanation of Ψ.[55]

Let us apply this schema to an example, ascribing to

x: the kidneys
s: the human organism
Ψ: survival
Φ: the cleaning of the blood

(When replacing the variables, one has to force the style a bit.)

The statement 'The function of the kidneys in the human organism is the cleaning of the blood' means according to our schema that 'The goal of the human organism is survival, and the cleaning of the blood by the kidneys is an essential factor in the explanation of survival.'

If we want to shed light on the function of a language or of elements of a language, we have to find appropriate substitutes for s, Ψ and Φ.

In so far as the function of language is concerned, I would propose the following:

x: a/the language
s: the human being
Ψ: social success
Φ: influencing others

'The human being has the goal to be socially successful, and influencing others by means of language is an essential element in the explanation of social success.'

There is an obvious alternative which, I think, is worse:

x: language
s: society
Ψ: communication
Φ: the exchange of thoughts

'Society has communication as its goal, and the exchange of thoughts is an essential element in the explanation of communication.'

Why should this variant be worse? Let us look at the variables one by one. The substitution of 'society' for 'the human being' adds a new problem to the explanation: what does it mean to say that a collective entity has goals, if it does not mean that the individuals in the collective have these goals? Collectivist concepts must be reducible to individualistic concepts, or they have no explanatory value. Reducibility in this context means being able to indicate how the statement about the collective can be constructed from the statements about the individuals. Statistically speaking, it can therefore be said that each German family has 2.3 children, because this is a statement based on the number of children of each individual. The statement 'The German people are striving for unity' (although the unity has now been achieved) is not allowed under these premisses. If it were advantageous for the society to communicate, without also being advantageous to the individuals, it would be difficult to explain how the custom of communication could have arisen; and even if it had been established 'from above' by some clever authority, to explain how it could have survived?

What about the remaining two variables Ψ and Φ? It is correct to say that the exchange of thoughts is an essential element in the explanation of communication. But if it is right to say that communication means trying to get people to do something by making them recognise that one wants them to do so, it follows that communication is a kind of influencing, and that the exchange of thoughts is a special case of making-someone-recognise. That is, this functional analysis would be almost circular, since the concept of the exchange of thoughts is included in the definition of communication. If we transform 'society' back to 'the human being' for the above reasons, the second variant would be equivalent to the platitude 'People want to communicate and language serves this purpose.' This is undoubtedly true. In the same sense that the function of scouring powder is to scour, it is the function of means of communication to communicate.

The function of a thing, as I wrote above, is its contribution to the functioning of a superordinate system, not its contribution to the functioning of itself. This means, however, that we have to find an answer to the question of communication's use for people. The proposal I just made is that communication (as a special form of influence) is useful in gaining social success.

The notion of social success will also be relevant in a later chapter. That is why I would like to prevent any possible misunderstandings at this point. In our present society, talking about social success suggests that one wants to say that somebody has 'made it':

a second car, a house in the country, a swing hammock. This is not what 'socially successful' means in this context. Here, striving for social success is understood as striving for everything concerning our social co-existence; the important and the unimportant, the enduring and the ephemeral. Included here are goals like influence, affection, food, power, attention; being understood, being read, being accepted, having a mate, and such like. I do not want to exclude the idea of status symbols that 'socially successful' usually evokes, but it represents only one of many forms of social success. As with biological fitness, social success cannot be substantially defined. The qualities that make a greenfly 'fit in' are different from those for a squid. Social success is the epitome of what we strive for in our social actions, of which communicative actions are a part. What counts as social success is different in a punk group than in a silent order of monks (see section 4.5).

Asking about the function of elements in a system is very different from asking about the function of the system itself. The clock has a function for human beings which is different from that of the hand of the clock for the clock. Again, not everything in a clock must have a function, and not every function of a clock's part must be directly linked to the function of the clock as a whole for human beings. Some clocks contain mechanisms that prevent their repair when they are defective.

Opinions diverge on the question of which elements in a language are functional for communication. Chomsky and his followers, for example, support the thesis that syntax is autonomous, which means that every natural language has an autonomous syntactic module which cannot be explained by semantic or pragmatic functions, and 'which cannot be reduced to any non-syntactic regularities'.[56] If we are dealing with elements of universal grammar, those parts of our faculty of language which are common to all languages, and which are based on our biological make-up, this has no bearing in our context. For what is common to all languages is also common to all stages of language evolution and immune to historical change. This module would change only when our biological make-up changes, and this goes well beyond any considerations of historical linguists.

Linguistic units can have many different functions, and one linguistic unit can have several at once. A certain pronunciation of an expression is firstly the phonetic realisation of this expression and secondly a signal of origin and social class. Language is for us not only a means of making oneself understood, but also of self-presentation in the broadest (and by no means only negative) sense. This is why we so easily make a judgment about the way in which someone speaks. If I hear a television evangelist say 'There ain't no passage to 'eaven from 'ell', I not only observe objectively that he drops his h's, I also immediately associate certain 'personal qualities' with it. Marks of linguistic behaviour are normally interpreted in a personal way. The language of a human being is (and is taken as) part of the person him- or herself. One can use words to flatter, show off, hurt, praise, insult, advertise, adapt oneself, attract attention, and, last but not least, make oneself understood. Some of these things can be done simultaneously, because communication is a multi-motive game that has many ends, all subordinated to influencing other people.

In what sense is an invisible-hand explanation of a linguistic unit's change functionalistic? It shows what special function triggered the change. Let us have another look at the pejoration of the terms for women.[57] Our explanation makes it clear that speakers of German do not only use the word *Frau* to refer to women, but also to play the game of gallantry; not only to be polite and deferential in a general sense, but to be gallant in a courtly–social sense. This is the function responsible for the pejoration.

This is to say that some functions of use can be self-destructive. Everything to do with distinctiveness belongs under this heading. But if many people make the same distinctive choice, what was once distinctive becomes normal and thus unfit to fulfil its function. Of course, this is only one of the reasons why the speakers of language feel compelled to modify their preferences of expression. Other cases will be discussed later.

What matters here is the following: to know why a linguistic phenomenon changes is to know what it is used for, as well as the function which is the basis for the expression's modification in the game of communication.

As an invisible-hand explanation of a linguistic phenomenon always starts with the motives of the speakers and 'projects' the phenomenon itself as the macro-structural effect of the choices made, it is necessarily functionalistic, although in a 'refracted' way.

One way to argue against the possibility of a functionalist explanation of language change is to say that it is not intended. Roger Lass writes, for example, that 'Change does not involve (conscious) human purpose';[58] for this reason, among others, he regards functionalist explanations as impossible. It is true that the change (or the new state after the change) is not intended, and quite often extremely 'unwelcome', and that 'in general, as I have already noted, the term *intention*, when used of languages, must be interpreted with care'.[59] However, 'conscious human purpose' is always 'involved'. One can say that the explanandum is a non-functional effect of functional actions. Once the point of an invisible-hand explanation has become clear, it is ultimately a terminological decision to call it functionalistic or not. That most of the instruments of our language are functional is not due to the fact that we as speakers produce all sorts of useful instruments, but because we avoid the ones which are not useful over and over again in favour of those which seem more useful to us. This process of selection and filtering creates teleonomy without finality: un-planned functionality.

4.4 MAXIMS OF LINGUISTIC ACTIONS

Depicting the structure of an explanation by the invisible hand makes it more tangible:

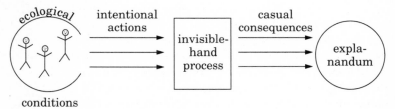

The diagram shows which factors play a role in the explanation of a linguistic phenomenon's change or its stasis. In a complete explanation, they all have to be taken into account. On the left of the box is the micro-level, on the right the macro-level. The micro-level is the level at which one can situate the actions of the individuals involved, plus the relevant circumstances of their actions; the macro-level is the language in a hypostatised sense. The box itself represents the cumulative process which functions as a bridge between micro-level and macro-level.

I would like to comment on the left side first.

If many people do arbitrary and disparate things which lack any common ground, one can assume that nothing interesting will emerge – in any case, no invisible-hand process. Invisible-hand processes emerge when many people act similarly in certain respects; or, in other words, when the actions of many show **relevant similarities** in at least one aspect. A thousand people can go from A to B with ten thousand intentions. A footpath will emerge only if their actions are similar in at least one aspect, that as much energy should be saved as possible. Among all the reasons, motives and intentions of their actions, only one is relevant for the explanation: the strategy of the shortest possible route.

A necessary condition for the emergence of invisible-hand processes is that actions demonstrate similarities. However, this condition is not sufficient, as there may be irrelevant similarities, those which leave no 'traces'.

One can capture the aspect of the relevant similarity of actions (following Grice's model[60]) in the form of maxims. I shall call them maxims of action.

A maxim of action represents a tendency to act in a certain way or a conscious or unconscious strategy of action. Its typical form is an imperative sentence. This imperative sentence should be chosen in such a way as *to make the action appear to comply with that imperative.*

Go from A to B in such a way that the route chosen is the shortest possible.

This is a possible formulation of a possible maxim which could play a role in the explanation of a path across the lawn. The way in which such a maxim of action is formulated gives no clue as to how the relevant similarities of the actions in question are actually established. The tendency of moving from A to B using the lowest consumption of energy may be due to our biological equipment or to rational deliberation; it may also represent a culturally acquired behaviour.

In our diagram, the three arrows pointing towards the box represent the relevant actions which are governed by one or several of such maxims of action.

I would like to point out two simplifications hidden in the preceding paragraphs.

First, it goes without saying that not *all* the members of a group must contribute to the emergence of the phenomenon to be explained. How large the contribution of the 'active' ones has to be, or actually is, depends on many factors – for example, the kind of phenomenon itself, or the 'ecological conditions', as I have called them in the diagram.

Second, it is not necessarily the case that all those who contribute to the emergence of the phenomenon act according to the *same* maxims. They could act according to equivalent maxims. The ecology of action is the sum total of the factors which influence the choice of an action. Actions do not take place in a vacuum. The acting agent is always exposed to a multitude of conditions and factors which can be of a restrictive nature, but can also open up possibilities for action. Primarily, the piano enables the pianist to play the piano, but at the same time it restricts the pianist by the way it is built. In every given situation of communication, the speaker of a language is confronted with restricting or enabling conditions of action. These conditions determine to some extent the choice of communicative means, given certain goals of action, but they also determine the goals of action and provide certain possibilities. We have to adapt if we want to communicate.

The ecological factors which influence the choice of linguistic means made by a certain speaker are partly linguistic and partly extralinguistic. The intralinguistic factors are those concerning the individual competence of the speaker and his or her expectations concerning the individual competence of the interlocutor. The hearer's real competence is not one of the factors influencing the speaker's actions, as he or she has no access to it. My hypotheses about your competence are part of my competence. Extralinguistic factors are, for example, social facts, facts about the material world, and possibly biological facts. However, it is not possible to distinguish strictly between intralinguistic and extralinguistic factors, as some social and biological factors influence linguistic competence directly.

All these ecological conditions have been traditionally called 'causes of language change', and it has normally been distinguished between intralinguistic and extralinguistic 'causes'. Our diagram clarifies the status of these so-called causes.

As indicated in section 1.3, language change can be planned without being an intentional phenomenon. The reason for this is clear now. A phenomenon of the third kind can, indeed, be planned as a phenomenon of the third kind. Under certain circumstances, one can arrange for the emergence of a desired invisible-hand process. We see this in the planning of national economy; whoever wants construction to boom can subsidise the interest rates for loans. Those who subsequently start building do not do it to stimulate the construction industry; that is, the stimulation of the construction industry is not an intentional phenomenon. However, those subsidising the interest rates did so to arrange the ecological conditions of action in a way to make people do things, the consequence of which is the stimulation of the construction industry. An example of a language policy modelled on market economy would be if homosexuals started to call themselves *fags*. It would obviously be their goal to get rid of the discriminating function of the word *fag* by stealing the term of abuse from 'the others'. From that point onwards, those no longer using the word as a term of abuse would not intend to cause a semantic change of the word *fag*, but they would in fact bring it about. It is clear that a word used by a certain group to characterise itself can no longer be used to discriminate against its members.

Even conscious language policy or language planning 'from above' cannot stop the invisible-hand mechanism. It only represents a factor – possibly a very effective one – in the ecology of the speaker's actions. There is nothing, neither a structural attribute nor a power or 'force', that has any direct effect on language. Every linguistic process has to go through the individual and must be explained on this basis. As Coseriu writes, there can be 'no external driving force of any kind that has any influence "on language", without going through the freedom and the intelligence of the speakers'.[61]

A maxim of action is a function which maps sets of ecological conditions into the realm of possible actions. It determines the choice of possible actions under certain conditions. Maxims of action are functions of action choices.

Let us have another look at the German example of the mid-nineteenth-century disappearance of *englisch* in the sense of 'angelic'. Again, $englisch_1$ represents the meaning 'angelic', $englisch_2$ the meaning 'English'. Going through the various stages of our diagram, I shall try to explain this disappearance.

I The **ecological conditions** to which a speaker found himself or herself exposed at that time were:

(a) That which could meaningfully be called $englisch_1$ was a (small) subset of what could meaningfully be called $englisch_2$.
(b) $Englisch_1$ and $englisch_2$ were homonyms.
(c) Around the middle of the nineteenth century, 'being angelic' was the ideal a woman aspired to; this led to an increase in the number of occasions on which $englisch_1$ was used.

(d) At the same time, England and English products attracted the attention of the public due to industrialisation and the resulting rivalry with Germany; this increased the number of occasions on which *englisch*$_2$ was used.

(e) conditions (c) and (d) together exposed a previously harmless potential for a conflict of homonyms.

(f) *Englisch*$_1$ is generally considered to be a derivation of the noun *Engel* (angel), thanks to the word-formation rules of German, which allow almost synonymous non-homonymous alternative derivations (e.g. *engelhaft*).

(g) condition (f) is not valid *mutatis mutandis* for *englisch*$_2$.

(h) Those who wanted to avoid being misunderstood (due to (b)–(e)) had the possibility (due to (f) and (g)) of avoiding *englisch*$_1$ but not *englisch*$_2$ in favour of alternative expressions.

(i) Due to (a), the chances of being misunderstood were greater for *englisch*$_1$ than for *englisch*$_2$.

II Given (a)–(i), the **maxims of action** which led to the disappearance of *englisch*$_1$ from the German language were:

M1: Talk in such a way that you are not misunderstood.
M2: Talk in such a way that you are understood.

M1 and M2 are not equivalent because being misunderstood is not the contradictory opposite of being understood. As we shall see later, each maxim makes a different contribution to the invisible-hand process.

III The **invisible-hand process** initiated by the avoidance of the word *englisch*$_1$ is of a relatively simple nature. Used less frequently, the word was on the one hand forgotten by those who once knew it; on the other hand, it was no longer learned by the next generation of speakers. This brought about a positive feedback effect. With fewer speakers having this word in their (active) vocabulary, fewer were able to use it, which led not only to the avoidance of the word but also to the inability to use it. This meant, however, that the ecological conditions changed for those who still knew the word. From then on, they avoided using the word *englisch*$_1$ even in situations where there was no risk at all of being *misunderstood*, because in view of the low frequency and the limited spreading of the word, the chance of being *understood* was slight.

IV The **explanandum** is the causal consequence of this process. The word *englisch*₁ disappeared from the German language. The 'laws' leading up to this result are extremely elementary.

L1: Words which are seldom used are rarely learned.

L2: If a hearer does not know the meaning of a word, his or her chances of understanding what a speaker means by the use of that word are much reduced.

4.5 STASIS AND DYNAMICS OF LANGUAGE

In order to say that *a thing* has changed, something about it must have remained stable, to guarantee the identity of that thing which one claims has changed. 'I still use *the same broom* I used ten years ago; I only had to change the handle once, and once I had to put on a new brush.' This statement is not completely absurd, although the current state of the broom has no more in common with its first state than two different brooms would have. If I had exchanged handle and brush simultaneously for another handle and another brush, it would no longer be 'the same' broom, not even if the two parts were identical with those it replaced. All this tells us something about our criteria for identity in diachrony. To talk meaningfully about change, there must be stability. Lüdtke[62] aptly calls this type of diachronic identity 'relay continuity'.

Stasis and dynamism are brought about by different types of maxims of action. There are maxims which, given a heterogeneous starting point, produce homogeneity; given a homogeneous starting point, they produce stasis. This is especially true of the maxim 'Talk in such a way that you are understood.'

To communicate implies (among other things) the wish to be understood. But if wishing to be understood results in stasis and homogeneity, how does the phenomenon of change occur at all?

'If a language is a systematic organism . . . and if its function is mutual understanding in the community in which it is spoken, then one should expect stability of it, as a system which fulfils its function adequately. However, the opposite is the case: the system changes.'[63] I consider this conclusion to be completely correct (contrary to Coseriu (1958/1973), where I found this quotation). An error is contained, however, in one of the two premisses: namely, that 'its function is mutual understanding'. Language has a multitude of functions, and if one should be stressed, it is the function of influencing others, to which 'mutual understanding' is subordinated (see section 4.3). Roger Lass writes: 'If language is many things other than a communication system, including a form of play, then change can occur, presumably, for reasons totally unconnected with communicative 'function'.'[64]

In ordinary language we often equate 'communicating' with 'talking with one another'. This is unfortunate, because in doing so we blur things which are relevant in this context. In a stronger sense, namely Grice's, communicating means 'saying something and meaning something by it'. What I communicate is therefore exactly what I mean. To mean is, according to Grice, intending in some complex way (which I will not comment on in detail here; see section 2.1) to make the other recognise something. That is, the other has understood what I meant if and only if he has recognised exactly that which I intended him to recognise. Putting it differently, understanding means recognising the speaker's open intentions. According to this *façon de parler*, communicating means 'openly intending to make someone understand something'. More liberal views about communication, such as those according to which one cannot fail to communicate,[65] are too simplistic to be useful in any linguistic analysis.

As we normally try to accomplish several intentions with one communicative action, there are several levels of incomplete understanding. If understanding means recognising *all* (open) intentions of a speaker, the contradictory opposite of understanding is recognition of *less than all* open intentions (i.e., failure to recognise some intentions). The contradictory opposite of 'understanding' is therefore 'partial understanding'. 'Not understanding' accordingly means 'to recognise none of the intentions'. Misunderstanding occurs if the addressee assumes that the speaker has intentions which he did not have; casually put, if he has 'understood' something the speaker did not mean.[66] One could thus have understood someone while at the same time misunderstanding him (having recognised all the speaker's open intentions, while presupposing some he did not have at all). It might be more reasonable to say that the addressee has understood the speaker if he has recognised all the speaker's intentions and did not assume any he did not have. In this case, the contradictory opposite of 'understanding' would be 'to understand partially or to misunderstand'.

If we consider the range of possibilities, from 'not understanding at all', to 'partially understanding', to 'understanding completely', along with the possibilities for partial and complete misunderstanding, the complexity of the facts dawns on us. But there is worse to come: in *communicating*, we do not *communicate* all the intentions we have. There are some intentions underlying our communicative act that we do not want to be recognised. There are others that we want to be recognised, but we do not want anyone to recognise this.

I would like to provide some examples, because the theoretical descriptions of speakers' intentions are usually much more complicated than the demonstration of such communicative and manipulative actions. As complicated as the theoretical descriptions may be, they belong to everyone's standard repertoire.

When I say to someone, *You look nice today*, I usually intend that person to recognise that I think that he or she looks nice today. It might also be that I intend to get them to share my opinion about their looks. However, if I also intend to ingratiate myself with them, I would certainly not want them to recognise this intention. The reason is that I can only succeed in this intention if it remains unrecognised. This is an example of an intention which is pursued in communication without being communicated itself.

Let us look at a more complex case. If small children want to show off, they usually do it in a very direct way, such as *My mum has a Jaguar* or *My dad earns a lot of money*. If adults want to give an impression of wealth, they have to do it in a more indirect way to succeed, such as: *The Jaguar dealer here is really very obliging*, or *We are in such a tax bracket that there is no reason to earn a few quid on the side*. If I say something like this, I intend the addressees to recognise that I have a Jaguar or a high income, but I do not intend them to recognise that I want to communicate just that. This is regarded as bad taste, and would therefore ruin my attempt to impress the others.

This means that we have to distinguish between open and hidden intentions, between the sense of an utterance and the sense it communicates. The sense of an utterance is the set of all intentions pursued with the utterance, whereas the communicated sense of an utterance is only that subset of intentions formed by the open intentions.

It often happens that precisely *that* intention which really matters in the production of the utterance will not be communicated (should not be understood).

Mutual understanding is thus not 'the function' of language, but at best one among others (although an important one). If it were language's only function, one would expect stasis rather than change, as Alarcos Llorach correctly points out. I would like to justify this claim here.

As indicated above, communicating (in a certain way) means getting intentions recognised, and understanding this means recognising these intentions. The maxim

(3) Talk in such a way that the other understands you.

means therefore (4) or (5)

(4) Talk in such a way that the other can recognise your intentions,
(5) Indicate your intentions in such a way that the other can recognise them.

What can I do to get you to recognise my intentions? I could hope that you might guess them correctly. But that would not be a very promising procedure. If we want to meet each other without having previously arranged a meeting place, it would not be rational to hope that we would meet by accident. If I would like you to recognise my intentions and you want to recognise them, we are in a situation analogous to those who want to meet. Coincidence is not impossible, but to set one's hopes on it is irrational.

The problem we are facing is the classical one of co-ordination. Such problems of co-ordination can be solved successfully only 'through the agency of a system of suitably concordant mutual expectations'.[67] The only rational way to meet you under the circumstances sketched out above, with a success rate greater than chance, would be for me to go to the place where I expect you would go if you wanted to meet me. In other words: I go where I think you would go (if you wanted to meet me). And where do you go? If you are rational, you go where you think I would go (if I wanted to meet you). Hence, my strategy should be:

I go where I think you would go if you were in my place.

This is the strategy we should choose if we wanted to meet without being able to arrange a meeting place.

Wilhelm von Humboldt seems to have seen that such a strategy (mutatis mutandis) plays a central role in communication. As a 'mental power' whose 'function is understanding', he proposes the following maxim.

Therefore, no one may speak to another differently from the way in which the latter, under similar circumstances, would have spoken to him.[68]

This is the strategy which one should follow if one wants to be understood. I would like to call it Humboldt's maxim. If our only goal in talking consisted in being understood, our maxim of communication would thus be

Talk in a way in which you believe the other would talk if he or she were in your place.

My thesis is that this maxim – a slightly modified version of Humboldt's own formulation of it – produces homogeneity if the starting point is heterogeneous and stasis if the starting point is homogeneous.

How is this possible? If you talked to me in my way, and I talked to you in your way, we would just exchange our ways of talking. How should homogeneity and stasis come about that way?

Humboldt's maxim functions in a more subtle way. How do I know how you would have talked to me if you had been in my place? I would know this from occasions on which you talked to me, among other things. But in doing so you were obeying Humboldt's maxim. Presumably, you talked to me as you thought I would have talked if I had been in your place. If I try to talk to you as you would talk to me under similar circumstances, I actually imitate how you talk when you try to talk like I talk when I try to talk like you talk, and so on. This is how a continuous alignment between our competences is brought about, and thus a stabilisation when this alignment has been more or less achieved.

I assume that this is one of the most fundamental maxims of communication. It is the strategy we use if we want to be understood. We sometimes apply this strategy even in situations where it is objectively foolish to act according to it. It would be foolish, for example, to apply it in situations of teaching and learning, in which the speaker should be a model for the addressees, enabling them to improve their competence. But since we have internalised Humboldt's maxim so strongly, we tend to talk to small children as they talk to us, and with foreigners we use broken English. In linguistics, this phenomenon is known as 'baby-talk' or 'foreigner-talk'.

There is yet another way through which homogeneity and stasis can come about: in every kind of adaptation strategy – communication according to the maxim

Talk in such a way that you are recognised as a member of the group,

or

Talk in such a way that you do not attract attention

and others which are similar. These are all variants of the simple maxim

Talk like the others talk,

(where 'the others' can obviously be a minority).

With the help of a computer program, Jules Levin[69] has modelled the maxim

Talk like the people around you.

He was able to establish that such a maxim can produce baffling structures. A shortened version of the argument will be presented in the following paragraphs.

It is Levin's goal to model the distribution of variants over a certain territory. The existence of two variants is presupposed as given. As an 'area', he chooses a square grid containing, for example, 55×55 unit fields. Each field has been allocated a certain value, 'black' or 'white'. The distribution of the values across the whole 'area' is random. The distribution of the 'language area' which has been created in this way is represented in Figure 4.1.

Levin developed a computer program[70] which simulates a certain interaction between the two variants. The value of each field can stay constant or change, depending on the value of the adjoining fields. Every field which is not at the border of the grid has eight neighbouring fields (including the diagonally adjoining ones). The program should roughly simulate the maxim 'Talk like the people around you'. A randomly chosen field, let us say a black one, has a certain chance of remaining black or of becoming white, depending on how many of the eight neighbouring fields are also black (or white). According to Levin's algorithm, a field surrounded by eight fields of equal value can have this value in the next run, whereas a white field which is surrounded by four white and four black fields has a 51 per cent chance of staying white.

The result of this simulation is astonishing. After only a relatively small number of runs, a structure starts to emerge which is bafflingly similar to a map of isoglosses (see Figure 4.6). Figure 4.2 shows the result after twenty repetitions. This structure is smoothed out in the following runs, and soon becomes stable (see Figures 4.3–4.5). It still remained stable after 10,000 repetitions.

Needless to say, such a model is a far cry from a 'realistic' model of language change. 'Although my students became convinced that the grid was a territory, the squares villages or individual speakers, and the two variants real language variants, I knew better', writes Levin.[71] 'I regard this as only a very primitive and abstract preliminary model that hopefully mimics linguistic interaction.'[72]

However, this model does have implications for certain aspects of our theory of language change. It demonstrates that the maxim on which the model is based creates a structure of homogeneous territories from a random distribution, and that the homogeneous structure thus created remains stable. The model demonstrates further, as Levin remarks correctly, that language change may 'be understandable on a grand scale as a kind of dynamic pattern emerging from simple and understandable interactive principles.'[73]

I call such interactive principles (i.e., maxims) which create homogeneity and stasis **static maxims**. Correspondingly, I would like to call maxims which create dynamics **dynamic maxims**. To this category belong the following maxims:

(6) Talk in such a way that you are noticed.
(7) Talk in such a way that you are not recognisable as a member of the group.
(8) Talk in an amusing, funny, etc. way.
(9) Talk in an especially polite, flattering, charming, etc. way.

The well-known principle of economy also belongs to this category:

(10) Talk in such a way that you do not expend superfluous energy.

Maxims (6)–(9) are profit-orientated. Maxim (10) concerns the costs. I assume that at least these two types of maxim exist, but I do not want to exclude the possibility of a more appropriate classification than one based on macro-structural effects. As the example of the maxim of understandability shows, a certain maxim cannot always be neatly allocated to one of the two types. On the one hand,

Iteration: 0

Figure 4.1

Iteration: 20

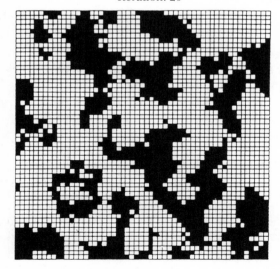

Figure 4.2

Iteration: 80

Figure 4.3

Iteration: 500

Figure 4.4

Iteration: 1,000

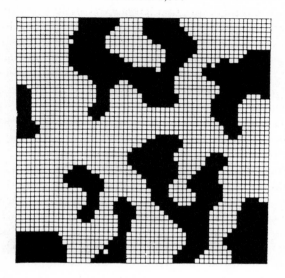

Figure 4.5

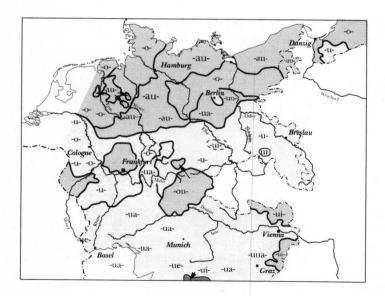

Figure 4.6

trying to be understood is mainly responsible for the fact that our language 'holds together', that languages spread when domains of communication increase their scope; on the other hand, this maxim is also responsible for the fact that, under different circumstances, words like *englisch* disappear from the vocabulary of a language. In conjunction with another maxim, the maxim of understandability is even responsible for a certain type of permanent change.

This has been well demonstrated by Helmut Lüdtke,[74] and I will discuss this phenomenon in more detail in the following chapter.

Under normal circumstances, we do not choose our linguistic means according to exactly one maxim. When we are talking, we try to kill several birds with one stone: we try to conform, attract attention, be understood, save energy. It is extremely rare that someone wants nothing but to be understood. If this should arise, the person in question would always use orthodox means, because every innovation puts understanding at risk. Those who want to be understood would act according to the expectations of others. Anything new is necessarily less expected. If I were ever in danger of drowning, I would shout the word *help* loudly and clearly. I would try neither to be creative nor to save articulatory energy. Some maxims are in conflict with each other; they contradict each other. If we nevertheless want to act according to two at once, we have to compromise. This, too, is no exception, but more likely the rule. To attract attention and be understood as well is one such typical conflict. It is a gamble between conforming and distancing, orthodoxy and innovation.[75] A typical example is advertising. The copywriter has to talk in a creative and funny way about boring things like toothpaste, flour, or washing powder to largely uninterested addressees, attracting attention while being effortlessly understandable.

Processes of evolutionary change can primarily be expected in areas where individuals experience shortages.[76] Scarcity means accelerated selection. In animate nature, selection processes are primarily stimulated by shortages in space, energy (sunlight, food, etc.), time, and sexual partners. Slight individual differences have favourable or unfavourable effects in the competition for scarce or desirable means. Those who are favoured have a higher probability of achieving a relatively higher rate of reproduction than those less favoured competitors. The effect is that those qualities that are favourable will be genetically transmitted to the next generation at a higher rate, something which will again favour the descendants – provided the environment stays the same. One can call fitness the probability of a type of individual's reproduction in a given environment. Hence, if variations change the fitness, evolution occurs.

Do we experience similar shortages in that part of life which we manage through our language? Yes, but there is one important difference. The shortages which we as communicators encounter do not only have a selective effect; they also increase the rate of variation. The reason is that variation in the domain of culture is not, as in nature, dependent on chance. It arises mainly through human creativity, which anticipates selection. And as we know, necessity is the mother of invention.

As communicators, we must be able to handle shortages of attentive listeners or readers, shortages in possibilities of publication (in the widest sense), shortages in time and energy on the part of the speaker, shortages in care, affection, and patience on the part of the addressee, shortages in social prestige and friends, even shortages in clients, buyers, voters, admirers, etc.

As part of our linguistic and communicative competence, we all use more or less good strategies to mastermind our communicative enterprises. To act always means to try to transform a relatively less desirable state into a relatively more desirable one. It goes without saying that this is also true for communicative action. The hyper-maxim governing our communication is therefore

Talk in such a way that you are socially successful.

What is considered successful differs from case to case, from situation to situation, from individual to individual, from group to group, and from addressee to addressee. The above hypermaxim is insubstantial. It has nothing to do with substantial features of social success (see section 4.3). It stands as an abbreviation for the (equally insubstantial) maxim

Talk in such a way that you are most likely to reach the goals that you set for yourself in your communicative enterprise.

Communicative goals can be to deceive someone, comfort a child, be read, convince, sell a car, be seen as intelligent, make someone laugh, make an acquaintance, be seen as taciturn, or be disliked by someone; in most cases, one of the subgoals is to be understood.

My hypothesis is that this hypermaxim can be broken down into submaxims, which can again be subcategorised into the two classes of stable and dynamic maxims. The maxim of economy,

Talk in such a way that you do not spend more energy than you need to attain your goal,

probably has a special status. It is undoubtedly one of the dynamic maxims. However, it is not primarily concerned with the attainment of the envisaged goal, but with the 'costs'. This means that our hypermaxim should possibly be modified in the following way:

Talk in such a way that you are socially successful, at the lowest possible cost.

The so-called economy principle demonstrates the validity of the hypothesis that shortages produce change. According to André Martinet's[77] wording, this principle implies that 'every given language changes in the course of time . . . because of the need to adapt itself in the most economical way to the needs of communication of the community which speaks it'. Based on this thought is the correct assumption that speakers usually communicate in a situation where there is a shortage of time or energy, something which tended to be overgeneralised in the past.

In a 'diachronic conflict' of a special kind, the maxim according to which we save articulatory energy clashes with the maxim according to which we talk in such a way as to be understood. Helmut Lüdtke has examined it and discussed its unintended consequences. In the following chapter I will present this theory of an invisible-hand phenomenon and try to classify it ontologically.

Chapter 5

Discussion

5.1 LÜDTKE'S LAW OF LANGUAGE CHANGE

In complete agreement with the position taken here, Lüdtke's theory stands in the tradition of methodological individualism. His explanations are explanations from the bottom up. He does not regard language as a thing, a given inventory, a sign system or such like, but as a 'certain procedure' adopted by human beings to communicate with one another. The instruments we use in communication have no logical existence prior to their use, but are the results of communicative enterprises. The type of language change he deals with in his theory 'emerges as an inadvertent, unconscious by-product of the coupling of free decision and the search for optimisation involved in linguistic activities'.[1]

This means that, to be understood, our communicative acts must have sufficient sound structure; Lüdtke calls this 'signal-negentropy'. Too little sound structure would hamper their chance of being understood by the addressee. An example should clarify this.

When I go to a pub in the evening, I say [ʔiːvnɪn]. Removed from that situational context, this noise would lack sufficient 'signal-negentropy' to be correctly understood in the sense I intend. If, in another situation, I were worried that I would not be correctly interpreted, I would have the possibility of providing my 'noise' with a bit more sound structure. I could produce 'noises' varying between [ʔiːvnɪŋ] and the full form [gʊd ʔiːvnɪŋ]. But I can only be so distinct. There is an upper limit – the full form. There is no similar lower limit. [ʔiːvnɪn] is already quite abbreviated, but [nɪn] would be enough under certain conditions.

Hence, we usually talk according to the maxim 'Talk in such a way that you expend the least amount of energy necessary.'

What does 'necessary' mean here? What one needs depends partially on social factors, but I would like to disregard those in this context. Focusing on the factors of pure transmission, 'necessary' is exactly as much articulatory effort as the addressee needs to identify the message correctly. Trying to hit this quantity exactly, however, would be a risky strategy, as only rather too little signal-negentropy would ruin the communicative enterprise. In communication, therefore, we rely on **redundancy**, a surplus of signal-negentropy which exceeds the absolute necessity for correct interpretation.

But too much redundancy is not good either. Too little redundancy is a danger to comprehension; too much redundancy risks losing the attention of the hearer. The strategy cannot be to save as much energy as possible, but to be as economical as possible and as redundant as necessary. The speaker is thus confronted with a management problem: controlling the amount of redundancy in accordance with the success rate of being understood by the addressee. Lüdtke calls this '**redundancy management**'.

However, as we have just seen, the articulatory possibilities have an **upper limit**. One cannot be more distinct than perfectly distinct. To increase redundancy beyond the acoustically possible, one must use lexical means. If I believe that my [gʊd ʔiːvnɪŋ] might not have the desired effect – perhaps because of the background noise – I could say, for example, 'I wish you a very good evening'. There are no upper limits to this type of lexico-syntactical expansion. There is no limit to long-windedness. However, there is a lexico-syntactical minimum. (One may only fall below it in telegrams and military orders.)

The management of redundancy is thus limited on two sides and open on another two. There is a lower limit of lexico-syntactical wellformedness and an upper limit of articulatory explicitness; conversely, there is no absolute upper limit to long-windedness and no absolute lower limit to articulatory sloppiness.

From this it is clear that lexical–morphological change is preprogrammed in a certain direction. Due to the fact that articulation has an upper limit but no lower one, linguistic units can only become shorter. Words wear out, as one could say colloquially. Given the maxim of articulatory energy-saving, forms which were once 'careless' abbreviations of full articulatory forms tend to become normal forms: new full forms, which then in turn undergo the same process of 'wear and tear'. *Hiu dagu* (on this day) became *hiutu* in Old High German, *hiute* in Middle High German, and has now become *heute*, which will probably become 'Late New High German' *heut*.

Extrapolating on this trend, one would expect to find that all lexical units reach a phonetic minimum at some stage. However, the facts show otherwise. The reason lies in what Lüdtke calls '**the principle of quantitative compensation**'. If, at some stage, the full form of a lexical unit – even explicitly articulated – has become so small that it no longer satisfies the redundancy needs of the speaker, it is increased by lexical means. The loss in sound is compensated for on the lexico-syntactical level. Those who think *heute* (today) is too small can choose to use *am heutigen Tag* (on this present day). And if *heute* is reduced to *heut* or an even shorter form, it is likely that *am heutigen Tag* would slowly increase in frequency until it becomes the normal form. This vision of the future for German is already a reality in French. Latin *hoc die* (on this day) became *hui* in Old French; this was lexically expanded in Modern French and became *aujourd'hui*, which, translated etymologically, means nothing other than 'on the day of today'.

If we extrapolate on this principle of phonetic shrinkage and lexical compensation, we arrive at the following result: in some future time there will be nothing but discontinuous sequences of minimal sound forms instead of lexical units. This, too, is contradicted by the facts. Lüdtke's '**principle of fusion**' explains why this is not the case. Linguistic units which tend to occur together as neighbouring units are no longer experienced as separate by the speaker–hearer (more notably as hearer). They are perceived instead as a single unit. A unit is nothing more than a set piece of speech which occurs with high frequency. An average speaker of French will no longer regard *aujourd'hui* as the prepositional phrase *au jour d'hui* (otherwise one would not find *au jour d'aujourd'hui* in French, meaning 'on this present day'). If, based on the principle of fusion, a new unit has emerged from the former 'neighbouring units in a morphological chain',[2] the whole process starts all over again. The principle of energy-saving, the principle of lexical compensation to safeguard comprehension, and the principle of fusion all concur to produce an infinite, directed and irreversible cycle:

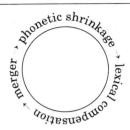

In this context, Lüdtke writes about a universal law of language change. This raises two questions concerning the ontological status of Lüdtke's claims:

1 Are we dealing with a universal phenomenon?
2 Are we dealing with a law-governed process?

These two questions are not equivalent. It is true that a positive answer to 2 implies a positive answer to 1, but the universality of a phenomenon in the cultural domain does not necessarily imply that we are dealing with a law-governed process. This is to say that if we are forced to answer the second question with *no*, the first one becomes an empirical question that we cannot answer. Now, Lüdtke illustrates the process he describes with a multitude of cases drawn from different languages, but in the face of the universality hypothesis, each new example is obviously only a drop in the ocean. As I cannot provide proof of the non-universality of the process – from which it would follow by *modus tollens* that the process is not law-governed – I would like to set the first question aside for the moment and concentrate on the second.

I think that it is misleading to describe the process observed and explained by Lüdtke as 'law-governed'; not, however, on the ground that '"laws" of relevant type do not exist' in the history of languages and because 'the enterprise of seeking them is doomed to failure', as Roger Lass[3] claims (as others with and before him), but because, in each case, the input data for the processes involve actions. Actions are not law-governed, but instead have law-governed consequences. To my mind, Lüdtke has shown how three invisible-hand phenomena can follow each other cyclically so that the output of each preceding process (no matter where the starting-point is placed) provides the decisive ecological input conditions for each following process and sets it in motion. In his more recent article, 'Esquisse d'une théorie du changement langagier', Lüdtke

himself calls the process described a *processus de main invisible*.[4]
However, the prerequisite for the start of each consecutive process
is always that the people continue to act according to the maxims
presupposed by Lüdtke. But even if one is sure that they will do so,
they will not do it according to a law. Lüdtke proposes to call the
'laws' he has formulated 'laws of the third kind', distinguishing
them in this way from natural laws on the one hand and laws made
according to a plan, such as tax laws, on the other.[5] Energy-saving
articulation necessarily leads to phonetic shrinkage. But it is not
necessary for people to articulate in an energy-saving way. If a
sufficiently large religious community were to emerge which regarded articulatory sloppiness as a deadly sin, the language of this
community would cease to change in accordance with Lüdtke's
theories. There are, supposedly, small linguistic communities in
the region of the Pacific in which the people formally agree upon
certain fashions of pronunciation.[6]

With his theory, Helmut Lüdtke has grasped something that
Edward Sapir called a 'drift'.[7] By 'drift', Sapir understood a long-
term, directed movement of a language or a family of languages.
Putting the cart before the horse, Sapir wrote: 'The drift of a
language is constituted by the unconscious selection on the part of
its speakers of those individual variations that are cumulative in
some special direction.'[8] But one cannot plausibly see where the
speakers should get the unconscious tendency to 'drift'. 'Who does
the monitoring', Roger Lass asks.[9] A drift is not the reason why a
certain event happens. Lüdtke has demonstrated in his theory that
there are certain principles which can, if followed under certain
circumstances, produce a 'drift'. In my interpretation, Lüdtke has
thus sketched a framework for invisible-hand explanations in
which singular historical events can be interpreted. The 'drift'
itself is something that should be explained, and Lüdtke has done
precisely that.

Let us return to the problem of universality and suppose that
Lüdtke's thesis, that we are dealing with a universal phenomenon,
is right. What arguments could one put forward to defend this
thesis, apart from the (probably unattainable) empirical proof that
it is true?

One obvious argument for universal phenomena in language is
always that they are genetically programmed. But can a 'drift' be
innate? Obviously not.

One should not stretch the argument for innateness too far; this has already been clearly pointed out by Jean Aitchison.[10] To say that something is so because God made it that way has always tempted us to give up the search for a better solution prematurely. According to Aitchison, linguistic universals can be roughly divided into two classes, inasmuch as they originate in two different ways. On the one hand, they can be directly innate. Our use of the vocal–auditory tract as a medium of communication, for example, is part of the genetic equipment of human beings. On the other hand, one cannot assume that our fear of lions is directly innate, although it would be a universal attribute of human beings. Our fear of lions is probably part of a much more general problem-solving strategy (approximately: 'Don't get into a fight with something stronger than yourself'). That all languages seem to have nomina, for example, could simply be due to the fact that 'the world in which humans live is composed to a large extent of separable objects. Obviously, we have to assume that there is some genetic determinism involved for humans to be able to recognize objects, but there is no need to claim that there is a language blueprint containing the component "noun".'[11] In summary, there are directly innate universals and indirectly innate universals, the latter being those that follow indirectly from innate principles and behaviour strategies that are not language specific.[12]

The cyclical drift described and explained by Lüdtke could be such an indirectly innate universal. The principles on which Lüdtke draws for his explanation are indeed of an elementary and non-language-specific nature:

1 *the principle of economy*: try to achieve the goals of your actions with as little energy as possible;
2 *the principle of redundancy*: when choosing the means to achieve your goals of action, choose rather too much than too little;
3 *the principle of fusion*: interpret sets of things which (almost) always occur simultaneously as units.[13]

The fact that these principles are of such an elementary nature warrants the (probably extensive) universal compliance with them. This does not make them laws, however. For nothing forces us human beings to behave according to our innate nature. One has to keep in mind that some of our cultural rules have precisely the 'task' of transforming our instinctive behaviour (as we have seen in section 3.1).

Explanations such as these, which use maxims, principles and strategies (or whatever one might call them) can shed some light on the hitherto somewhat mysterious concept of 'drift'. As Lüdtke's theory demonstrates, a drift comes about when speakers are faced with certain ecological conditions, arising from (among other things) the respective state of their language and the problems inherent to the success of communicative enterprises, and react over and over again according to the same maxims. In principle, there is no difference between a morphological drift as described by Lüdtke and a semantic drift such as the continuous pejoration of the courteous expressions for women. 'Overall, then, it seems likely that historical linguists have a major role to play in future research into the principles underlying language.'[14]

5.2 ON THE THEORY OF NATURALNESS

'The greatest revolution that has occurred in recent methodology, at least in historical reconstruction, is what can be subsumed under the rubric of *naturalness*', wrote Bailey in 1980.[15]

That same year, Lass arrived at a very different conclusion. Under the heading 'Why "naturalness" does not explain anything', he wrote: '. . . since the theory says that "optimisation" is to be defined in terms of increasing "simplicity", then "common" = "natural" = "optimal" = "simple". . . . What it expresses is the blinding tautology that nature tends towards the natural.'[16] Two evaluations of the same theory can hardly be more controversial. Is there an explanation for this? I think so; and my explanation is, bluntly put, as follows.

Research under the heading of 'naturalness' has achieved a host of interesting, sophisticated, and valuable results. Principles were formulated, historical drifts and trends were discovered, empirical observations were reorganised from the point of view of naturalness, and so on.

But so far, theoreticians of naturalness have failed to develop a consistent theory of naturalness. It is not clear what it is they claim to explain, nor how they want to attempt explanation.

Even the central concept of naturalness itself has not yet been provided with any binding explanation. No one has ever tried, to my knowledge, to integrate the concept of naturalness into a higher-order theoretical framework.

In other words, the controversial evaluation of the concept of naturalness is due to the fact that it has proved to be very productive

and stimulating on the one hand, but on the other, that it was never
theoretically elaborated, enabling it to resist sharp criticism such as
that put forward by Lass.

I would like to demonstrate this by discussing two central points:
the concept of naturalness and the explanatory claims of the theory
of naturalness. First, however, I will try to present the *theory* of
naturalness as congenially as possible.

The theory of naturalness has three main domains: phonology,
morphology and, in recent times, syntax. The theory found its
beginnings with Stampe's paper, entitled 'The Aquisition of
Phonetic Representation', in which a concept of natural phonology
was introduced. These ideas were taken up again in the 1970s and
proved useful in the field of morphology, mostly due to the efforts
of Dressler, Mayerthaler, and Wurzel. My presentation of the theory
of naturalness will be based mainly on the theory of natural
morphology, but for all these areas the basic ideas are the same.

The fundamental idea of natural morphology, in Wurzel's words,
is 'the assumption that morphological phenomena can be evaluated
by their naturalness or markedness'.[17] The central concepts 'natural'
and 'marked' are generally used as inverse synonyms: the natural is
the unmarked and the unnatural is the marked. A continuum exists
between the poles 'natural' and 'unnatural' – 'a graded scale of
maximally natural/unmarked to maximally unnatural/marked'.[18]
One assumes that there exists, in the different levels of language,
a series of principles that determine the direction of language
change – so-called 'universal principles of morphological naturalness (markedness principles, preference principles)'.[19] Such principles are, for example, 'the principles of constructional iconicity,
the principle of morphosemantic transparency, . . . and the principle of system congruity',[20] to name only a few. As a means of
explanation, let us consider an example of each of these principles.

The principle of constructional iconicity, for example, corresponds to the fact that normally the plural form of a noun is longer
than its singular form; that is, 'more things' is iconically mapped as
'more phonemes'. 'It appears that the type *boy* – *boy-s* is maximally
iconic, the type *goose* – *geese* minimally iconic, and the type *sheep* –
sheep noniconic.'[21] The plural of *sheep* is consequently marked, that
is, unnatural; it is therefore more likely that *sheep* – *sheeps* will
emerge than *boy* – *boy*, and more likely that children will form the
incorrect plural *sheeps* than the incorrect plural *boy*.

The principle of morphosemantic transparency states that a code following the principle 'one function – one form' is better than when one form is responsible for many functions: accordingly, the Old High German forms *zungun* – *zungono* ('the tongues' – 'of the tongues') are less natural than the corresponding New High German *die Zungen* – *der Zungen*, because in Old High German the inflectional forms -*un* and -*ono* must specify both number and case, whereas in New High German the article *die* or *der* specifies case, and the ending -*en* specifies number.

The principle of system congruity assumes that the morphology of a language is determined by certain 'system-defining structural properties'.[22] Forms that do not correspond to these properties tend to be replaced by system-congruent forms. German (like English) has, for example, basic-form inflection rather than stem inflection. This means that inflectional endings are attached to the basic form of the word and not to its root, as in Latin. Now, there are many words in German that come from Latin or Greek and whose plurals are formed according to the principle of stem inflection: *Aroma* – *Arom-en*, *Dogma* – *Dogm-en*. The plural forms *Aromen* and *Dogmen* tend to be replaced by forms more appropriate to the prevailing system: *Aromas* and *Dogmas*. *Aromas* is already tolerated, while *Dogmas* is still seen as incorrect.

According to the theory of naturalness, these various principles can come into conflict. Usually there are conflicts between 'morphology, with its semiotically motivated naturalness principles, and phonology, with principles that are motivated articulatorily or perceptually'.[23] An example should clarify this. Unstressed [e], as in the German *haben*, is spoken as [ə] due to phonological principles of naturalness – thus [haːbən]. This reduction results in the assimilation of the nasal [n] to [m]; [haːbən] becomes [haːbm]. The sequence [bm] is further reduced to [m], again because of the principles of naturalness, so that finally the maximally natural form [haːm] emerges. This is in fact the current, normal, colloquial pronunciation of the word *haben* (compare, for example, Latin *habent* > Spanish *han*). But the paradigm *ich* [haːbə] – *wir* [haːm] contradicts, for example, the principle of morpho-semantic transparency. That is, 'an increase in phonological naturalness involves a decrease in morphological naturalness'.[24] Due to such conflicts, new developments constantly emerge, so that the language never comes optimally and naturally to rest.

What ontological status is given to such principles? 'Natural principles (of any component) have the character of universals that are tendencies, or more strictly speaking, they are *Gesetzmäßigkeiten* having the character of tendencies, i.e., statistical laws in the epistemological sense of "law".'[25] These principles are, then, universal tendencies and statistical laws, and in conformity with natural laws. Wurzel formulates the connection between language change and these principles as follows: 'For natural morphology language change follows from the continuous interaction of the naturalness principles: thus, it results directly from the very nature of the language system.'[26] From these two statements taken together, it follows that language change is the result of the interaction of universal tendencies that have the character of statistical laws. This statement clearly shows that something is wrong with this theory. The universal tendencies mentioned above are tendencies of change. To say that language change follows from tendencies of change is simply wrong. An established tendency is not the cause or the trigger of change; it is, rather, a descriptive generalisation of established phenomena of change. Tendencies and statistical laws allow so-called trend extrapolations, but not conclusions. A defining characteristic of trend extrapolations is the very fact that they are forecasts without explanatory power. The correctly formulated connection between language change and the principle of naturalness is as follows.

Natural morphology, in the fields where it has been applied, has established that language change is directed; that is, it follows certain tendencies. Some of these tendencies are universal. They can come into conflict, which prevents the language system from reaching a standstill.

This statement is no mean result! But it provides no explanation. Exactly these tendencies and their universality are in need of explanation. As earlier stated, I will now clarify the concept of naturalness, and in connection with this, attempt to make several constructive suggestions.

The concept of naturalness itself is normally defined in a circular, tautological way, but in any case very unclearly; that which is usual is unmarked is simpler is natural. For Mayerthaler, 'a morphological process or structure is natural if it (a) has a wide distribution and/or (b) is acquired relatively early and/or (c) is relatively resistant to language change or frequently the result of language change, etc.'[27] In a similar fashion, Wurzel characterises naturalness by using the concept of system adequacy, and notes that 'a morphological phenomenon is all the more natural and therefore less marked, the more it corresponds to the structural attributes that define the respective language'.[28] As the attributes that define the system of a language are the predominant, usual ones, this definition, too, only means that the usual is the unmarked and the unmarked is natural. Natural changes, Wurzel adds superfluously, 'consist of nothing but the decrease of the . . . marked phenomena, which are replaced by unmarked or less marked phenomena'.[29] As unmarked is equated with natural, this observation means that natural changes go from the less natural to the natural. This tautology finds its best expression in the following quote from Stein: 'Any departure from optimal natural structure is more marked and less natural',[30] from which one can immediately infer that 'any departure from natural' is 'less natural'.

Apart from the tautological definition of naturalness, it is above all the lack of clarity of this concept which makes understanding difficult. Are we dealing here with linguistic structures, diachronic regularities, or processes that can be called 'natural', as Wurzel and Mayerthaler seem to suggest, or are we dealing with 'factors of a prelinguistic infrastructure in the domain of cognition, reception and behaviour',[31] as Stein proposes in some of his formulations? In other words, it is completely unclear what should be termed natural. On which level of observation should this concept be used: on that of linguistic structures and phenomena, of diachronic processes, or of individuals' communicative actions? I would like to propose an answer, but for the moment I will dwell a little longer on the destructive part of my exposition.

Another open question concerns the explanatory claim. According to the theoreticians of naturalness, what should and what can be explained? Should single cases of language change be explained? For example, why the Latin *inbibere* became *imbibe* in English, or that *in between* will presumably become *imbetween*; or why *Aromas* will become the plural of *Aroma* in German, rather than *Aromen*? Should existing trends or 'potential directionalities' be explained, or 'the logical gap between the tendency in the individual and the unidirectionality of tendencies in groups'?[32] Is it the trend that one wants to explain or does one assume that the trend explains the individual case? Fitting quotations for each of these positions can be found, and frequently, contradictory examples in one and the same work.

In my opinion, the theory of naturalness can have explanatory power if certain principles are followed. I would like to take the example that Lass used to show 'why naturalness does not explain anything' and use it to show how naturalness could explain something.

Lass chooses a clear case of naturalness and attempts to bring this presumed explanation into explicit form: the consonant combination [nb] commonly becomes [mb], a well-known process of assimilation. This serves as an example of a possible portion of an explanation based on the theory of naturalness – why the Old High German *einbar* (*beran*, 'to bear') became the Middle High German *eimber* and New High German *Eimer* ('bucket').

According to Lass, an explanation of such a process of assimilation based on the theory of naturalness would be reconstructed as follows:

C_1 a sequence [nb]
L_1 [mb] is 'easier than' [nb]

E   [nb] > [mb]
E does not follow deductively, of course; and L_1 isn't really a law.'[33]

Lass shows in a second step that this 'explanation' is not improved by the introduction of a so-called 'statistical law'. The revised version:

C_1 a sequence [nb]
L_1 [mb] is 'easier than' [nb]
L_2 It is overwhelmingly (very, quite, etc.) probable that, given a choice, speakers will choose 'easier' articulations over 'harder' ones.

E   [nb] > [mb][34]

Naturally, the explanation becomes neither better nor weaker because of the so-called 'statistical law'. E remains what it was: a *non sequitur.* This is because statistical laws are not laws that allow conclusions, but rather generalisations. For example, the fact that 90 per cent of chain smokers die of lung cancer does not explain, of course, why the chain smoker Max died of lung cancer. His death was caused by chemophysical processes in his lungs, not by the statistics. His death confirms the statistics, but the statistics do not explain his death. 'Singular counter-instances do not falsify probabilistic theories',[35] as Lass correctly concludes. This explanation is therefore only a pseudo-explanation without explanatory power.

Lass's analysis is correct. But the theoreticians of naturalness brought this unfavourable judgment of their theory upon themselves by failing to specify their explanatory claim. Legitimately, Lass chose to deal with the most problematic variant: he assumes that the theory of naturalness claims to explain the individual case, such as the change of *einbar* to *eimber*. But this is precisely what such a theory cannot do. What it can do, however, if it is properly conceived, is explain the trend. In other words, the theory of naturalness explains the trend, but the trend does not, for the aforementioned reasons, explain the individual case. Such an explanation of a trend could look like this:

C_1 There are sequences [nb]

C_2 [mb] is easier to articulate than [nb]

C_3 The implementation of [nb] as [mb] does not normally hinder the communicative goals of the speaker.

L_1 Of the alternatives available to them, people naturally choose those that promise the highest subjective net benefit.

L_2 If the majority of individuals in a population deviate frequently and repeatedly from the prevailing convention, and deviate in the same way, a shift in convention towards the deviation will occur.

E   A shift in convention from [nb] to [mb] usually occurs.

This deduction has two advantages over the former: it is valid and has explanatory power. It cannot predict whether *in between* will become *imbetween*, but it explains the trend. The falsifying case is not the individual case, but rather a speech community with a language for which the conditions C_1–C_3 and the laws L_1–L_2 are valid, but the trend does not occur. This explanation contains two laws, which – and this is of crucial importance – do not apply to language, but rather to human behaviour (L_1) and to the logic of the concept of convention (L_2). Needless to say, the individual conditions and laws, especially L_2, can be more precisely formulated. The weak expression 'usually' in E comes from the condition C_3, which is important; from uncertain conditions and 'hard' laws comes a 'weak' explanandum. Nothing, however, comes from uncertain laws.

What are the principal differences between Lass's reconstruction of the explanation of the change from [nb] to [mb], according to the naturalness theory, and my proposal? There are three:

1 Lass's reconstruction of the explanation attempts to explain the individual case, whereas mine explains the existence of a trend.

2 My explanation distinguishes strictly between the micro-level of individual behaviour and the macro-level of language structures.

3 My explanation is dependent upon the principles of methodological individualism, which means that the explanation is based on acting individuals, not languages, structures, processes, or collectives.[36]

The strict distinction between micro-level and macro-level makes it possible to leave behind the unfortunate terminological duplicate *natural* and *unmarked*, which is essentially to blame for the circularity of the definitions mentioned earlier. In my opinion it would be sensible to reserve the term *natural* for the micro-level and (*un-*) *marked* for the macro-level. Such a terminological differentiation makes possible the formulation of the empirical and non-circular hypotheses that the natural behaviour patterns of speakers, in the sense of 'known principles of human nature', generate unmarked structures, under certain conditions, on the level of language. Such an assumption about naturalness is contained in L_1 of my explanation. In this way, naturalness (human behaviour) and markedness (linguistic structure) can be independently defined and systematically related to each other.

Modified in this way, the theory of naturalness does not contradict the postulate that every explanatory theory of linguistic change must have the form of an invisible-hand theory. The explanation I suggest is an invisible-hand theory that includes the assumptions of the rational-choice theory. The basic idea of the rational-choice theory is as follows.

Human actions are determined by three factors: their goals, possibilities, and restrictions. Humans are able to put those alternatives of behaviour that are aimed at a certain goal into a hierarchy, according to their subjectively expected net benefit. This means that when people have a choice of various alternatives to reach their goal (which is almost always the case), they will choose that alternative which promises to result in the highest subjectively expected net benefit. This is as true for Mother Teresa as it is for a masochist or a New York stockbroker. They do not differ in the rationale of their actions, but rather in their assessment of the benefit of those actions. The net benefit of an action is its benefit minus its costs. Because the acting subject is not necessarily completely aware of the objective range of behavioural possibilities and conditions, the net benefit must be restricted to that which is subjectively expected. The more advantageous the relation of costs to benefits is for the acting subject, the more justified the choice of that action. A choice of action is considered to be explained when it is shown to be subjectively optimal, based on the acting person's knowledge of the conditions. (The rationality of sub-optimal choices, so-called 'satisficing', cannot be dealt with in this context.)[37] So much for the basic assumptions of the rational-choice theory; let us return to the theory of naturalness.

As early as the nineteenth century, linguists knew that the development of language had something to do with the strive for articulative economy and the principle of least effort.[38] Language grows 'according to the natural laws of wise economy',[39] as Jakob Grimm wrote in 1819. This is one of the traditions in which the theory of naturalness stands. For this reason, the area of phonology and morphology is seen as the principal domain of explanatory attempts based on the theory of naturalness. These are the areas in which the consequences of the 'law of wise economy' are mostly evident. Because the subject is more aware of the factor of benefit optimisation than that of cost saving, the danger of speech that has been abstracted by the speaker, speech that hypostatises the language, is particularly acute. But lowering costs is not the goal of the speaker; whoever wants to do this can simply be silent. In communication, as in all other action, the determining factor is the optimisation of the balance between costs and benefits. Helmut Lüdtke's theory (section 5.1) has already made this clear. The factors of cost and benefit that go into the choice calculation of linguistic means in a communicative act can be presented in the form of a tree:

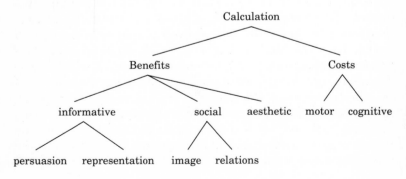

This model shows that, under benefits, one must differentiate between informative, social, and aesthetic usefulness, and under costs between motor-related and cognitive costs. Informative usefulness can mean either persuasion or representation. Social usefulness can be in terms of either image or relations. All in all, five factors of benefit and two of cost go into the choice of linguistic means. Beneficial factors are persuasion (an expression that is convincing or understandable), representation (the most accurate expression), aesthetics (stylistic formulation), image (the choice of 'prestige' words), and relations (polite expressions). Cost factors are motor-related (energy needed for articulation, word length, etc.) and cognitive (memory capacity, perception). If we assume, for example, that the desire to make a positive impression on the conversation partner is no less natural than the attempt to lower articulation costs, we must come to the conclusion that the explanatory range of the theory of naturalness does not have to be restricted to phonology and morphology, but that it can also be applied to semantics and syntax. In accordance with this concept, the objects of the theory of naturalness are exactly those phenomena of language change that are caused by the maxims of universal human behaviour ('the principles of human nature') and which, depending on the initial linguistic condition, produce different effects from language to language.

5.3 DIACHRONY OR SYNCHRONY?

The theory of maxims and of their role in the process of the invisible hand can shed some light on the relation between synchrony and diachrony. But first let us have a brief look at the use of these two terms in today's linguistic jargon.

It is well known that we owe the conceptual version of these two dimensions of language, or the analysis of language, to Ferdinand de Saussure. However, this distinction is admittedly older than its terminological determination.[40] Even up to the present day, it is controversial what this distinction should in fact distinguish. Some see in it predominantly ontological predicates, used to designate two 'ontological states' of a language; others would like to see them as methodological predicates used to designate different aspects of linguistics itself and different research perspectives.[41] 'De Saussure did not engage in ontology, but methodology. . . . This is why the distinction between synchrony and diachrony does not belong to a *theory of language* but to a *theory of linguistics*', claims Coseriu.[42] What Saussure was really engaged in has become rather unclear and controversial, since the name 'Saussure' has come to designate two different things: Ferdinand de Saussure on the one hand and the authors of the *Cours de linguistique générale* on the other. It is well known that these are not one and the same. The *Cours* was compiled by two Swiss linguists, Charles Bally and Albert Sechehaye, and purports to reproduce the thoughts that Saussure expressed in the lectures that bore the same title. However, the authors themselves did not attend these lectures. Their 'sources' were students' lecture notes and their own linguistic knowledge as renowned linguists of their time. It is therefore no surprise that they combined (intentionally or not), under the name of Saussure, their own theories with this 'reconstruction' of the lectures, based on sketchy lecture notes which themselves contained interpretative distortions. I do not want to get involved here in an effort to reconstruct[43] the theories held by Saussure himself. Our general understanding of Saussure's dichotomy and thus of the use of the terms 'synchrony' and 'diachrony' in our present linguistic jargon is in any case based essentially on the version put forward in Bally and Sechehaye's *Cours*. This version seems indeed to favour the methodological reading, linked to the recommendation always to distinguish quite clearly between the two levels, and the tendency to give priority to synchrony.

We adopt the synchronic perspective to study the state of a language, abstracting its change or dynamics; we adopt the diachronic perspective to study two or more temporally different states of a language. 'What diachronic linguistics studies is not relations between coexisting terms of a language-state but relations between successive terms that are substituted for each other in time.'[44]

Let us look again for a moment at the tentative explanation (put forward in section 4.4) of the disappearance of the word *englisch* in the sense of 'angelic' from the German language. To refresh our memory, it had the following form: given the particular linguistic and extralinguistic circumstances (a)–(i) which prevailed during the middle of the nineteenth century, communication according to the maxims M1 and M2 had to bring about the invisible-hand process described, which, according to the laws L1 and L2, led necessarily to the 'extinction' of the word $englisch_1$.

Are we dealing here with a statement made from the point of view of synchrony or diachrony? Rephrasing this question in more general terms, does a theory of change belong to the field of synchronic or diachronic linguistics? If we look again at the definition by Bally and Sechehaye, we observe that the answer can be either 'both . . . and' or 'neither . . . nor'. Now, if a question admits two contradictory propositions as answers, we can be sure that something is amiss with the concepts involved. In this case the conclusion is inevitable that the concepts 'synchrony' and 'diachrony' are not suitable for dealing with problems of language change. They are basically concepts which belong to a theory of the history of language, not to a theory of change. The concepts 'state (of being)' and 'history' are very different from those of 'stasis' and 'dynamics'. 'The past is the repository of that which has irrevocably happened and been created';[45] whatever belongs to history is static, but the place of dynamics is the present. A theory of change is not a theory of history, but a theory of the dynamics of a 'state'. An explanation of this type seems able to fulfil the claim for an 'integrated synchrony'[46] made by Coseriu in 1980 in his article 'Vom Primat der Geschichte'. Its task would be to define the manner in which 'the functioning of language coincides with language change'.[47]

The problem of language change – of a phenomenon of the third kind – is indeed not a historical problem. Whoever compares the purchasing power of the dollar at time t_1 with its purchasing power at times $t_2, t_3, \ldots, t_n$ is engaged in a diachronic study and compiles in this way a history of the dollar's monetary value. However, this method does not construct a theory of inflation. To explain the decrease in purchasing power over a certain span of time, a theory of inflation is needed but such a theory is not developed by generalising historical descriptions of purchasing power. It has already been pointed out by various authors that the problem of change is not a historical one. Carl Menger, for example, called it a problem of '*theoretical* social research';[48] Eugenio Coseriu called it a 'rational problem'[49] and Friedrich von Hayek wrote: 'Yet the problem of the formation of such structures is still a theoretical and not a historical problem, because it is concerned with those factors in a sequence of events which are in principle repeatable, though in fact they may have occurred only once.'[50]

The dichotomy between 'synchrony' and 'diachrony' does not really concern issues of becoming and change, because we are dealing with concepts designed for language in the sense of *ergon* and not in the sense of *energeia*: concepts used to characterise observations about language in the hypostatised sense. Thus we arrive at another problem which, on closer inspection, is related to the problem of synchrony and diachrony.

5.4 CHOMSKY'S I-LANGUAGE

Should linguists conceptualise and investigate language as language faculty, or should they, disregarding the speaker, consider language as a relatively autonomous entity? The debate concerning this question has re-appeared in the last few years.

Humboldt is well known for having first posed this question. The way in which he tackled the problem was by asking whether language should be considered a product or a capacity. He tended, as we know, to favour the latter definition: 'We must look upon language, not as a dead *product*, but far more as a *producing*.'[51]

In a different passage he expresses himself even more forcefully. Language itself 'is no product (*Ergon*), but an activity (*Energeia*).'[52] This insight had little effect on practical linguistics, and Coseriu was therefore correct in saying, 'This claim is often quoted, but in most cases only to be forgotten quickly, fleeing back to language as *ergon*.'[53] However, I believe that, in most cases, we are not dealing with flight but with a work requirement. What should a linguist working on a dictionary, a history of a language, the grammar of an individual language or a teaching manual do with those wise words that language is not a product but far more an activity, that is, 'that language proper lies in the act of its real production'?[54] Whatever language 'really' is, it is most useful to act as if it is an *ergon* (at least in most linguistic enterprises). In other words, the hypostatisation and reification of language is *in most cases* not an epistemological mistake but a practical necessity. But this is not true in all cases. An exclusively *ergon*-orientated approach is misplaced wherever questions about genesis or production come into focus. This seems to apply most essentially to generative theory and to the theory of language change. These are also the fields in which the question posed by Humboldt is again under discussion today, albeit under a different guise.

According to generative theory, all competent speakers have a certain linguistic knowledge at their disposal which enables them to generate any number of sentences and understand any number of sentences. This linguistic knowledge, composed of several interrelated and interacting components, is called grammar. It is assumed that only part of this grammar has to be learned during childhood; according to this theory, we are born with certain grammatical abilities. They are innate to humans, part and parcel of our biological equipment and thus universal. This innate part of our linguistic knowledge is called 'universal grammar' (UG). 'UG may be regarded as a characterisation of the genetically determined language faculty. . . . as a theory of the "initial state" of the language faculty.'[55] It is believed that, without this assumption, one cannot explain why all healthy children of this earth, regardless of which language they have to acquire, regardless of their intelligence and more or less regardless of the social environment, are able to acquire the language of their surroundings in such a short time, although the linguistic data with which a child is normally provided by its surroundings are extremely restricted and deficient. A child is able to accomplish this feat at an age when it is still quite unable to learn other similarly complex skills. (A child can, for example, construct counterfactual conditionals before it is even able to draw a circle on a piece of paper!) One assumes that this innate part of our linguistic knowledge does not so much consist in positive rules as in constraining principles. (Our legal and moral systems, for example, do not tell us what we are allowed to do, but what we should refrain from doing. It would be highly uneconomical and practically unlearnable if we were to codify what is allowed, because the domain of what is allowed is infinite.)

Hence the child constructs on the basis of innate principles and linguistic experiences an internal grammar, which is in some way mentally represented. According to more recent terminology, this mentally represented grammar is called I(nternalised)-grammar.[56] The language specified by such an I-grammar (the set of all sentences which can be recognised as being grammatically well formed by such an I-grammar) is called – according to this terminology – I-language. Important is that if, by way of example, a human being has learned a poem by heart, he or she has a mental representation of this learned poem; but this representation is not related to the poem as the I-grammar is related to the I-language, since what belongs to the I-language and what does not is determined by the respective I-grammar. In the case of the poem, on the other hand, the poem is logically primary.

A traditional linguist could agree with the argument up to this point. However, he or she would probably point out, 'What you Chomskians tell us about I-grammar and its relation to I-language is all very well and good. But this is only of marginal interest to me as a linguist, the reason being that it is not the task of the linguist to examine what is in a child's head; what should be of interest is the English language! And this exists independently of what is represented in your head or mine. A grammar of the English language is something altogether different from the grammar that human beings have in their heads.'

The dream of our fictional traditional linguist would be to establish the E(xternalised)-grammar of an E-language. According to this version of the world, the E-language is of course given, and the E-grammar is derived from it.

To this, a Chomskian would reply, 'What you call 'the English language' is a rather adventurous construct. Strictly speaking, this is not even a linguistically relevant category. To call something a language or not depends largely on political and sociological criteria.[57] Incidentally, a language is either something that is in fact "mastered" by someone (in this case, where your E-grammar of this language coincides with the I-grammar of a competent speaker of this language), or in your sense, something that is in fact not "mastered" by any empirical person (in this case, the language in your sense is something to which nothing in the real world corresponds).' Chomsky himself says, 'If you are talking about language, you are always talking about an epiphenomenon, you are talking about something at a further level of abstraction removed from actual physical mechanisms.'[58] In another passage he writes that 'the notion of E-language has no place in this picture. There is no issue of correctness with regard to E-languages, however characterised, because E-languages are mere artefacts. We can define 'E-language' in one way or another or not at all, since the concept appears to play no role in the theory of language.'[59]

I do not want to pursue the description of this quarrel any further. Instead, I would like to link the concept of a language as a phenomenon of the third kind to the I–E dichotomy.

For representatives of generative theory, the I-grammar is the real object of enquiry in linguistics. It is the only thing that has a real material existence. 'Grammars have to have a real existence, that is, there is something in your brain that corresponds to the grammar. That has got to be true.'[60] I-language is, so to speak, the 'externally' observable manifestation of I-grammar. It provides the linguist with the empirical data for the reconstruction of the I-grammar that generates it.

In this context, that part of the I-grammar which is regarded as innate is of special interest. It is common to all humans and thus to the grammar of all possible (natural) languages. This is why this part of I-grammar is called universal grammar. Research into the universal principles of our language faculty is of special value for two reasons: first, it is interesting in itself to know something about the organisation of the human mind; and second, it can explain some structural properties of our language (be it I or E). An explanation which deserves that name must be based, by necessity, on general laws or principles, as shown in section 4.2. If one intends not only to describe adequately the rules of a language, but to explain why they are as they are, the biological organisation of our mind represents an adequate explanatory foundation.

In my opinion, the way in which the proponents of generative theory make I-grammar their exclusive object of enquiry is a mistake. As this leads only to a limitation of their own field of research, it is quite harmless, as long as the generativists do not have the majority in the scholars' realm. It is easy to appreciate the usefulness of such self-limitation. A speaker's competence thus becomes a (physical?) attribute of the person. 'We suggest that for H to know the language L is for H's mind/brain to be in a certain state.'[61] Statements about grammar are interpreted as 'statements about structures of the brain'. From this it follows that 'Statements about I-language . . . are true or false',[62] and this in the strict sense of these terms. One has thus finally reached what linguists could only dream of for a century. 'UG and theories of I-languages, universal and particular grammars are on a par with scientific theories in other domains. . . . Linguistics will be incorporated within the natural sciences.'[63] As if overnight, through pure re-interpretation of research activity, the human and social sciences have become natural sciences; linguistics is now 'on a par' with the natural sciences!

The mistake consists in assuming that everything that can sensibly be said about the grammar of a language is said when its I-grammar has been described completely and adequately. Thus, Gisbert Fanselow and Sascha Felix, for example, take pains to argue that the assumption that language is a system of conventions, which emerges 'as if by itself through the so-called "invisible-hand process"'[64] is inappropriate, or at best, superfluous.

The argument that the above assumption is inappropriate runs as follows: conventions are necessarily arbitrary. 'In principle, the concept of convention therefore always implies the possibility that conventions might be violated.' Children know the language of their environment, but not by convention, because 'children have no choice'. Hence, 'It is extremely questionable, however, if, from this point of view, language acquisition and language use can be called a convention',[65] because 'Of necessity, everyone learns and uses the language of his environment; the question about convention and potential alternatives does not even arise in this context.'[66] This argument makes use of Frege's 'principle of the non-distinction of the distinct'.[67] Whether the English language represents (as a whole or in parts) a system of conventions is quite different than whether it is a convention that small children learn the language of their environment. Children do not learn their mother tongue because it is 'common practice' to do so, but because they are 'designed' that way. It is therefore indeed not a convention that 'Germans speak German or the French French',[68] although it is a convention to call what they speak 'German' or 'French'. It is true, however, that the object of their language acquisition is largely of a conventional type. In other words, what they learn is conventional, but that they learn is genetically determined.

This is the inappropriateness argument put forward by Fanselow and Felix. Now let us look at the superfluity argument. It runs as follows: if a language is a convention, 'the object of the convention must finally be a grammar.'[69] Now, one might think 'that the convention consists purely and simply in the fact that . . ., for example, all speakers of German have a mentally represented . . . I-grammar, which, in its central parts, would be the same for all individuals and would thus allow linguistic communication among them.'[70] If, however, the convention consisted 'in the possession of the same I-grammar . . . the convention could be completely reduced to the I-grammar; i.e., a complete and adequate specification of the I-grammar would at the same time be a complete and adequate characterisation of the convention'.[71]

This is the argument. Its internal validity depends on the extent to which one can resolve the lack of clarity which is hidden in the authors' concept of convention. Does the object of the convention consist in the sameness of the I-grammars, or do the authors mean that the object of linguistic knowledge (the I-grammar) is of a conventional nature? In the first case, nothing at all is reduced, because a specification of several (or all) I-grammars results in a theory about the linguistic knowledge of the speakers in question, but not in a theory about the sameness of this linguistic knowledge 'in central points'. In the second case, one could indeed claim a partial reduction. The object of the convention would indeed be comprised in a 'complete and adequate specification of the I-grammar', but not, however, the conventionality of the object.

Now, a hardened generativist could quite naturally say, 'I am not at all interested in the question of conventionality! I am interested in universal grammar, which is by definition not conventional but inherited.' This entails, however, the sacrifice of a condition of adequacy which is normally applied to linguistic theories.

Let us assume a speaker uttered the following sentence: *First there was dancing, then going home, then sleeping.* I will assume that the speaker of such a sentence does not violate any principle of universal grammar. He simply does not know that *going* and *sleeping* are not used as gerunds in such a context.

It is usually not the goal of linguistic theorising to describe the I-grammar of linguistic eccentrics,[72] but that of a speaker 'who knows his language perfectly', as Chomsky put it back in 1965.[73] Of course, Chomsky cannot do without idealisations in 1986. He is not interested in the I-grammar of any particular person, but only in 'the case of a person presented with uniform experience in an ideal Bloomfieldian speech community with no dialect diversity and no variation among speakers'.[74] The language of the 'hypostatised speech community . . . [should] be taken to be a 'pure' instance of UG'.[75] The idealisation is only shifted. In the past (1965), the idealised speaker was the object of enquiry; today, he is apparently a human being like you and I, but lucky enough to have learned to speak in a completely ideal 'hypostatised' speech community. This only means, however, that Chomsky is interested exclusively in a speaker whose I-grammar is *in conformance to convention.* But something's conformance to convention does not mean that it is identical with convention. Each of us participates in the convention of English, but none of us covers it completely. Hence, there is no one whose I-grammar is such that a 'complete and adequate specification' of this grammar would be a complete and adequate specification of the object of grammatical conventions in English.

In so far as I-language is concerned, every speaker is a competent speaker, because, as we have seen, the I-language is nothing more than just that set of sentences which is permitted by the I-grammar that generates it. A competent speaker of English, on the other hand, is someone whose I-grammar generates an I-language that is in conformance to convention. It is in conformance to convention if and only if it is a subset of that E-language which is generated by an E-grammar; that is to say, by the universally and conventionally valid principles and rules of a speech community.

Obviously, a language in the sense of a speech community's language is at a 'further level of abstraction' than the I-language, and a language is indeed an epiphenomenon of the actions that generate it. But there is nothing dishonourable in being an epiphenomenon. In the domain of culture, epiphenomena are often most interesting. Inflation is an epiphenomenon of our economic actions; religions are possible epiphenomena; the already mentioned footpath and traffic jams are epiphenomena: so are languages, in the hypostatised sense. One should be aware of what one sacrifices by intentionally leaving out the abstractive step between individual actions based on individual competence and the invisible-hand phenomena that result from them. First, the already mentioned concept of individual competence's conformity to convention is sacrificed, and with it an adequate concept of language acquisition, because language acquisition is based on the innate principles of universal grammar and the experiences resulting from communicative success and failure (active as well as passive). Through the experience of success and failure, and everything that lies in between, a child learns how to extract that which is conventionally valid from the multitude of linguistic input or intake from its community. Chomsky has hinted at the fact that innate linguistic knowledge is a filter for possible languages, as noted by James Hurford, who then continues to say, 'I wish to point out that the arena of use is also a filter.'[76]

Second, in sacrificing the above mentioned step of abstraction, one abandons the study of language change. Using Chomsky's I–E-dichotomy, we can distinguish between I-change and E-change. In doing so, we note again that E-phenomena cannot be reduced to one or several I-phenomena. For example, from the observation that the word *englisch* in the sense of 'angelic' has disappeared from the E-lexicon of the German language, and thus from the E-grammar, it does not follow that this word has disappeared from anyone's I-lexicon and thus from any I-grammar. From the observation that a change has taken place in my I-grammar, it obviously does not follow that a similar, equivalent, or any change at all has taken place in the E-grammar.

In other words, I-change is neither necessary nor sufficient for E-change to occur, and E-change is neither necessary nor sufficient for I-change to occur. I-change has nothing to do with language change, and language change is not something that happens in the head of a speaker. 'The distinction between I-language and E-language is useful in that it invites linguists to ask what the actual object of their study is. But a legitimate answer to this question can be "either" or "both".'[77] For questions concerned with language change, the only possible answer is 'both'. The reason is, to put it in Chomskian terms, that to explain language change is to prove that a phenomenon of E-language is an epiphenomenon resulting necessarily from the widespread use of I-grammars by the members of a speech community under certain historical conditions. It goes without saying that the use of an I-grammar implies knowledge that goes beyond the knowledge specified by the I-grammar. Chomsky himself stresses this point. As long as we have not answered the questions about 'how we talk' and 'how we act', he writes, 'it would be quite correct to say that something very important is left out . . .; I not only agree, but insist on that'.[78] However, it seems to me that the generativist overlooks the fact that E-language itself is a framework in which speakers make use of their I-grammar and in which they acquire and modify it.

5.5 POPPER'S WORLD 3

The generativists really cannot be blamed for their self-limitation. They are entitled to regard their form of linguistics as part of 'cognitive psychology and . . . in the end even as part of human biology'.[79] What is troubling, however, is the theoretical imperialism so often connected with this position, as if this research programme were identical with 'linguistics'. 'The theory of particular and universal grammars, so far as I can see, *can be sensibly regarded only* as that aspect of theoretical psychology that is primarily concerned with the genetically determined programme that specifies the range of possible grammars.'[80]

In contrast to the Chomskian position, it is sometimes claimed that language is a World 3 phenomenon. 'Languages are clearly in a sense more abstract realities than individual competences; if one were to put it in Popperian terms, one would say that a language belongs to World 3, whereas an individual's knowledge of it belongs to World 2', writes James Hurford[81] in a discussion of

Chomsky's I–E-dichotomy. Roger Lass writes in a similar context: 'If
. . . languages are "in" any world at all, it's . . . something like
Popper's "World 3".'[82] Therefore, according to Lass in a more
recent work, what we need is a 'theory of history for World 3
objects'. He provides the following reasons for this claim: 'I am
suggesting that it is reasonable to consider language histories in at
least some of their aspects as autonomous objects, long-term
morphogenetic scenarios whose locus is something like a Popperian
World 3.'[83] Popper, too, regards languages as part of World 3.

The external similarity between 'World 3' and 'phenomena of
the third kind' is pure coincidence. But it is nevertheless enlighten-
ing to compare the theory of the three worlds with that of the three
kinds of phenomena. That will be the object of this section.

Karl R. Popper divides our reality into three worlds:

> First, there is the physical world – the universe of physical entities
> – . . .; this I will call 'World 1'. Second, there is the world of
> mental states, including states of consciousness and psycho-
> logical dispositions and unconscious states; this I will call 'World
> 2'. But there is also a *third* such world, the world of the contents
> of thought, and, indeed, of the products of the human mind; this
> I will call 'World 3'.[84]

Popper thus postulates besides the outer 'world of physical objects'[85]
and the inner 'world of subjective experiences' another outer world,
which is linked to our inner world by a special tie, but is nevertheless
an outer world, namely that of the 'products of the human mind'.[86]
To this world belong first and foremost the products of consciously
planned mental activity, such as scientific theories, hypotheses (true
and false ones), and works of art. Popper focuses mainly on theories
and hypotheses. But language, too, is part of World 3. It has a special
importance in this world. 'One of the first products of the human
mind is human language. In fact, I conjecture that it was the very
first of these products, and that the human brain and the human
mind evolved in interaction with language.'[87] Popper obviously
recognises that language is not a human product, created according
to a plan. 'World 3 objects are of our own making, although they are
not always the result of planned production by individual men.'[88] In
a table with the title 'Some Cosmic Evolutionary Stages', 'human
language' is situated in the next to last stage, together with
'Theories of Self and of Death'. In the last stage, one finds 'works of
art and of science'.[89] Both stages together form World 3. It seems

reasonable to suppose that the next to last stage differs from the last stage in so far as those products of the human mind that belong to the former are not 'the result of planned production', whereas those belonging to the last and highest stage are mental artefacts that have been planned and created. Be this as it may, both types of 'products' belong to World 3.

The things that inhabit World 3 have one important quality: they are relatively autonomous. They are products of the mind, but

> nevertheless, they have a certain degree of *autonomy*; they may have, objectively, consequences of which nobody so far has thought, and which may be *discovered*; discovered in the same sense in which an existing but so far unknown plant or animal may be discovered. One may say that World 3 is man-made only in its origin, and that once theories exist, they begin to have a life of their own: they produce previously invisible consequences, they produce new problems.[90]

Although the objects of World 3 are human products, they lend themselves to new discoveries about themselves over time. This is certainly true for languages, and many linguists owe their existence to this fact.

Another important attribute[91] of World 3 objects is the fact that they have a 'real' existence.

> Many World 3 objects exist in the form of material bodies, and belong in a sense to both World 1 and World 3. Examples are sculptures, paintings, and books, whether devoted to a scientific subject or to literature. A book is a physical object, and it therefore belongs to World 1; but what makes it a significant production of the human mind is its *content*; that which remains invariant in the various copies and editions. And this content belongs to World 3.
>
> One of my main theses is that World 3 objects can be real . . . not only in their World 1 materializations or embodiments, but also in their World 3 aspects.[92]

In a dialogue with Eccles, Popper chooses as an example Mozart's *Jupiter* symphony: it is neither identical with the score nor with Mozart's own inner acoustic experiences while he composed it, nor with a performance, nor with all performances taken together or the sum of all possible performances. 'This is seen from the fact that performances may be good or less good, but that no performance can really be described as ideal.'[93] I refer to this example in detail because one can learn something about a language's type of reality from it. The *Jupiter* symphony is an object of World 3, '*a real ideal object* which exists, but exists nowhere, and whose existence is somehow the potentiality of its being re-interpreted by the human minds.'[94]

What does Popper understand by 'real'? Something is real when it can have an effect. 'We accept things as "real" if they can causally act upon, or interact with, ordinary real material things.'[95] Elsewhere he writes that 'interaction with World 1 – even indirect interaction – I regard as a decisive argument for calling a thing real'.[96] In this sense, language in the hypostatised sense is real, too. 'World 3 objects are abstract . . ., but none the less real; for they are powerful tools for changing World 1.' Already expressed in the idea of a tool, objects of World 3 have no direct effect upon the physical world, but 'only through human intervention, the intervention of their makers; more especially, through being grasped, which is a World 2 process, a mental process, or more precisely, a process in which World 2 and World 3 interact'.[97] Language is a World 3 tool used to change World 1 by means of World 2. 'The only tool that seems to have a genetic basis is language.'[98]

The human being as a physical object is naturally part of World 1; the mind and consciousness are part of World 2. The type of effect that World 3 has on the human being as part of World 1 and World 2 deserves special consideration. A human being is not born as a self. 'It seems to me of considerable importance that we are not born as selves, but that we have to learn that we are selves; in fact, we have to learn to be selves. This learning process is one in which we learn about World 1, World 2, and especially about World 3.'[99] The self is 'anchored'[100] in World 3 and thus in language. 'I have described World 3 as consisting of the products of the human mind. But human minds react, in their turn, to these products: there is a feedback.'[101] We are the users, changers, and creators (in a correctly interpreted sense) of language, and in turn, language has an effect on our acts of use, change, and creation. 'The social character of language together with the fact that we owe our status as selves – our humanity, our rationality – to language, and thus to others, seems to me important.'[102]

I have presented the theory of Popper's three worlds, and especially of World 3, in some detail, because it seems to me that one should understand its central points if one wants to use its terminology. Handy terms are easily misused when they are torn from the theoretical context in which they were defined and inserted into other theories.

The attraction of such a theory for historians of language and theoreticians of language change is that it makes language autonomous and real. The theory of World 3 supplies a philosophy that enables us to conceptualise an object like language, which is abstract, ideal, and hypostatised (remember the *Jupiter* symphony), as something (relatively) autonomous and really existing. It also has one decisive advantage over the world of platonic ideas. 'World 3 has a history; this is not the case for the Platonic world.'[103]

Let us consider the use Roger Lass has made of the concept of World 3. He believes, as a historian of language who wants to explain change, that he is left with adopting either the perspective of the speaker or that of a god ('God's-eye view'). He thinks that the first perspective is 'fundamentally wrong',[104] and therefore chooses the second. (Incidentally, Lass's God's-eye view does not seem to be that of an omniscient god; otherwise he could have looked into the hearts of the speakers!)

Lass argues that *'Languages are objects existing in time*, not timeless or momentary bodies of personal knowledge. Therefore they cannot be insightfully described – even at particular points – without reference to both their past and their future.'[105] Even a descriptivist, exclusively interested in synchronic description, must take history into account to achieve an insightful and complete description. 'Languages have an existence in some sense independent of that of their speakers: that is, they have *traditions*; perhaps more accurately, they *are* traditions.'[106]

However, speakers of a language are normally unaware of the history of their language. From this it follows 'that wherever we ought to be looking for the grounds for explanation, or even a preliminary ontological characterization, the inside of a single speaker's head isn't the place'.[107] The single speaker lacks the big picture; 'the participants in the pattern ... are not sources of information about what their behaviour actually means in a larger perspective'.[108]

I quite agree with Roger Lass on all these points. Let us look back at our simple example of a phenomenon of the third kind, the so-called 'traffic jam out of nowhere' (section 4.1). Such a traffic jam comes about because every driver, following the car in front, reacts to the person braking in front according to the maxim: 'I'd rather brake a bit too hard than not enough.' In this way, speed is reduced from vehicle to vehicle until it reaches zero. This example clearly demonstrates the correctness of Lass's theory: such a traffic jam is a real, autonomous entity which cannot be explained by looking exclusively at the knowledge of the participants and adopting their perspective. Those who get stuck in the traffic jam do not know how it came about and those who produced it do not know that they have. Every single driver lacks the 'historical' perspective which would be necessary to explain the traffic jam or even to describe it adequately.

But what is the advantage of 'the God's-eye view'? Now, I do not know Lass's religion. The omniscient god knows everything, as already mentioned; but Lass does not seem to refer to this type of god. What he means is a perspective 'from above' which excludes access to the view of the individuals; similar, perhaps, to traffic wardens in a police helicopter who are not gifted with empathy. The information they have is evidently not enough to understand what is going on 'down there'. To understand what is happening, they must do what traffic observers do automatically: establish a relation between the view from above and the inner view of the individual actors and make a connection between the two. Only then will they recognise the traffic jam as an epiphenomenon of every driver's urge for safety, and their explanation will then be an invisible-hand explanation.

Lass draws the following inappropriate conclusion from his correct diagnosis: 'What we may need is an intelligible approach to an "ontology of pure form", or a "theory of history for World 3 objects".'[109]

I am not quite sure I understand the 'or' in this statement. Is it there to indicate that there are two different approaches, either the ontology of pure form or a theory of the history of objects belonging to World 3? Or is the second clause meant to be a commenting paraphrase of the first? I suspect that this statement should be taken in the paraphrase sense. In this case, however, we are dealing with a very superficial interpretation of what World 3 should be. A theory of the history of an object belonging to World 3 should capture precisely that feedback process which exists between the minds and consciousness of the individuals and their products. My self is a product of the language, and I am (together with countless others) that language's 'creator'. Constructing a theory of the history of objects belonging to World 3 which would take this feedback process into account would, however, be something very different from an ontology of pure form. Such a theory should couple the view 'from above' with the internal view of the actors.

Natural languages are phenomena of the third kind and they are objects belonging to World 3. However, the set of possible objects belonging to World 3 does not have the same extension as the set of possible phenomena of the third kind. The two categories are formed according to completely different criteria. The objects of Popper's three worlds differ – casually put – in the material they are made of. Phenomena of the first, second, and third kind differ – again, casually put – in their production methods.

The objects of World 1 are physical objects, those of World 2 inner experiences, and those of World 3 ideas, theories, hypotheses, and the like. Phenomena of the first kind exist by nature, those of the second kind are products which are planned and fabricated by humans, and phenomena of the third kind are non-intentional, causal, cumulative consequences of human actions.

One cannot infer an object's production method from its material, and there is no way, either, to infer the latter from the former.

Certain combinations are impossible. The following matrix illustrates this. A possible combination has been symbolised by '+', an impossible one by '–'.

	World 1	World 2	World 3
natural phenomena	+	+	–
artefacts	+	+	+
phenomena of the third kind	+	–	+

This matrix tells us that there are no natural phenomena in World 3, that there are artefacts in all three worlds, that all three kinds of phenomena exist in World 1, and that there are no phenomena of the third kind in World 2.

The first row is obvious. As World 3 is the world of products of the human mind, and as natural phenomena are by definition not human products, World 3 cannot contain any natural phenomena. As to the second row, one might be in doubt whether there are artefacts in World 2, the world of psychological states. I believe that humans are able to produce feelings, fantasies, emotions, and such like voluntarily, and that it is appropriate to regard such experiences as artefacts. The allocation of values in row 3 is based on the fact that objects of World 2 as inner experiences are necessarily of an individual nature, whereas phenomena of the third kind are brought about by the actions of many.[110]

Two things emerge from this matrix. First, it contains neither identical columns nor identical rows, which shows that each of the two classification systems makes distinctions that the other cannot. This demonstrates that one cannot replace the other, but only supplement it.

Second, this matrix contributes something to the solution of the question concerning the primacy of I- and E-phenomena (see section 5.3). I can have a theory in my head and then publish it. An object of World 2 thus becomes an object of World 3. The theory is externalised, so to speak. I read a book and I adopt a theory; an object of World 3 thus becomes part of my World 2. By contrast, language as a phenomenon of the third kind cannot emerge in me and then be 'externalised' as an object of World 3. But I can partially make my own a phenomenon of the third kind – a language, a religion, a moral system, and such like. That is to say, given a language in the Chomskian sense (the set of sentences which can be generated by the I-grammar of a person or which can be judged well-formed by it), the inner states as part of World 2 are primary. The set of sentences defined by an I-grammar, be they uttered or not, is derived from it. A language as a phenomenon of the third kind is primarily an object of World 3, an object that can be partially internalised by a human being. The following is true of every individual human being: the existence of a language in this sense is independent of the fact that he or she is a speaker of this language. The I-grammar of a real, existing (non-ideal) speaker who has acquired language in a real (non-idealised) speech community should normally be a partial internalisation of a language existing as a phenomenon of the third kind in World 3, based on innate faculties and principles and altered by some idiosyncrasies.

Chapter 6

Conclusion

6.1 LANGUAGE CHANGE AS AN EVOLUTIONARY PROCESS

In this chapter I would like to address the question of the extent to which language evolution represents a case of (socio-)cultural evolution and what the mechanisms underlying such an evolutionary process could be. In this context, 'language evolution' does not mean the development of human language or languages from animal proto-forms, but the historical evolution of language.

Language evolution in this sense necessarily implies stasis as well as change, as already pointed out in section 4.5. Historians of language have traditionally focused on the aspect of change, perhaps tacitly assuming that 'Where nothing changes, there is nothing to be explained'. To my mind, there are no objective grounds for holding this view. There is, for example, no less need to explain the fact that the West Germanic *Satzklammer* (the rule that in a main clause with complex predicates, the finite part of the predicate must be in second position and the other parts of the predicate at the end of the sentence) has maintained itself in German, Dutch, and Afrikaans, than to explain the fact that it has completely disappeared in English and is almost gone in Yiddish (with the exception of sentences with prepositional objects).[1] The motto, 'If we do nothing, everything remains the same', does not work in language. If we 'do nothing', language no longer exists. But everything does remain the same if we do not change our preferences of expression. If we maintain or change them, we make in both cases a (mostly unconscious) choice, and the one is no less mysterious than the other. 'It may be', writes biologist John Maynard Smith, 'that the search for the causes of constancy in human affairs may prove as fruitful as has the comparable study of homeostasis in biology.'² The 'evolution of language' should therefore include both stasis and change.

The use of the word 'evolution' for social and cultural phenomena often arouses distrust, for two reasons. First, there is the general suspicion that the natural sciences are being inappropriately imitated. Second, there is the danger that one might be classified with social Darwinists. As both worries are not totally unfounded – which one can see by looking at the history of linguistics – I would like to comment on them briefly to prevent misunderstandings.

The desire shared by many linguists to be a member of the illustrious circle of natural scientists has driven some to dream up rather grotesque theories. I demonstrated this in section 3.2 by discussing the examples of Max Müller and August Schleicher. Chomsky's own works and those of his followers clearly show that this wish is still alive today (see section 5.3). I therefore want to stress that, when I say a theory of the development of language is an evolutionary theory, I do not thereby claim to present a theory belonging to the natural sciences.

Coseriu writes: 'One should note, for example, that the human sciences still have not found a concept to replace the bothersome and inappropriate concept of *evolution*: cultural objects have a *historical development*, not an "evolution" like natural objects.'³ Elsewhere he points out, 'The system does not evolve in the sense of an "evolution", but is *created* by the speakers in accordance with their expressive needs.'⁴

I am in fact in good company with my use of the expressions 'evolution' and 'genetic' in reference to the cultural object of language – even from Coseriu's point of view. 'If . . . we conceive of language-making as successive, we must base it, like all becoming in nature, upon a system of evolution.'⁵ These words were written by Wilhelm von Humboldt; elsewhere he stresses that the 'true definition' of language can 'only be a genetic one'.⁶

My thoughts on the matter stand in a sociological tradition which has also influenced biological theory. In his *History of Biological Theories*, Emil Rádl points out Bentham, Smith, and Malthus as forerunners of a Darwinian theory of evolution.

There was this new and magnificent idea of a **household of nature**, in which animals and plants have the status of members of a society, of citizens of nature . . . . It would be hard to understand why Darwin could have had such an influence on sociological thinkers, did we not know that his own theory was itself a **sociology of nature**, that Darwin projected onto nature the then dominant ideal of the English state.[7]

'Just as Adam Smith was the last moral philosopher and the first economist, Darwin was the last economist and the first biologist', wrote Simon N. Patton in 1899.[8]

With this, we come to the second danger: suspicion of social Darwinism. Those sociologists who tried to project Darwin's theory onto society were bad biologists and bad sociologists both. They used Darwin's metaphors of the 'struggle for survival' and the 'survival of the fittest' to justify racism and imperialism with the veil of science. They succeeded in doing so, mainly because they took the metaphor of struggle literally to prove that wars and oppression were somehow laws of nature; they also surreptitiously re-interpreted the theses of the 'survival of the fittest' as meaning the 'survival of the strongest'. The result of such an adaptation were statements like this: 'Lasting good can only be achieved in this world by struggle and bloodshed. As long as injustice exists in this world, the sword, the gun and the torpedo boat are parts of the evolutionary mechanisms of this world, blessed like any other of its parts', or 'Nature only wants . . . the best race to govern . . .. This is the law of nature.'[9]

'Those social scientists', wrote von Hayek, 'who, in the 19th century, needed Darwin to learn what they should have learned from their own predecessors, did progress in the theory of cultural evolution a great disservice with their "social Darwinism".'[10] But von Hayek probably misjudged the social Darwinists in assuming that they wanted to learn. It was not their intention to further the progress of a theory of cultural evolution; on the contrary, they wished to strengthen the acceptance of a certain colonial and racist policy by means of a justifying ideology.

To my knowledge, the influence of social Darwinism was negligible in the field of linguistics. It is true that Max Müller, too, used the metaphor of the struggle for survival, but without any Darwinistic implications: 'A struggle for life is constantly going on amongst the words and grammatical forms in each language. The better, the shorter, the easier forms are constantly gaining the upper hand, and they owe their success to their own inherent virtue.'[11] We find the same metaphor in the work of August Schleicher, this time with a clear tinge of social Darwinism.

He believed that he could observe how 'during historical periods
. . . species and genera of speech disappear, and how others extend
themselves at the expense of the dead', and that 'in the process of
the struggle for existence in the field of human speech . . . the
descendants of the Indo-Germanic family are the conquerors in the
struggle for existence', and that, as far as languages are concerned,
'the preservation of the higher organisms in the struggle for
existence' cannot be denied.[12]

My own attempt at conceiving linguistic development as an
evolutionary process is in no way driven by the wish to project a
model borrowed from the natural sciences onto an object belonging to the cultural sciences. On the contrary, I wish to apply a
genuinely cultural model, that of the invisible hand, to the study of
language. It is worth pointing out that there is only a small step
from the theory of the invisible hand to the concept of evolution,
historically as well as systematically. The theory of evolution in the
domain of animate nature can serve only as a heuristic model,
relying on 'the fruitfulness of analogical thinking, properly controlled' – as Gerard, Kluckhohn, and Rapoport point out in their
essay 'Biological and Cultural Evolution'.[13]

On what conditions can one be completely justified in calling a
process of historical evolution an evolutionary one? There are
three:

1 The process should *not* be a **teleological** one; that is to say, we
should not be dealing with a process which is carried out in a
controlled fashion to achieve a preset goal. This does not mean,
however, that evolutionary processes cannot have a certain direction. But on no account must they have a certain direction, not even
in the domain of animate nature.[14] The implementation of ortho-
graphical reform is thus not an evolutionary process, even though
it might take place over a period of biological time (and although
evolutionary subprocesses can take place within it).

2 It must be a **cumulative** process. 'By evolution', write Gerard,
Kluckhohn, and Rapoport, 'we mean the cumulative process of
small changes.'[15] That is, we are normally dealing with a process
which is brought about by populations, not by a single individual. I
say 'normally' because there are borderline cases. A trowel takes on
a specific shape because it is always used by the same person with
the same habitual movements. This shaping process is cumulative

and not teleological. Is it evolutionary? Or the development of my individual competence during my adulthood; is this an evolutionary process? To my mind, it would be terminological arbitrariness to exclude such one-man processes, although such processes are surely not prototypical in so far as evolutionary processes are concerned.

3 The dynamics of the process must be based on the interplay between **variation** and **selection**. Excluding random effects, this is the case when there are, generally speaking, alternatives which are differently suitable for a certain purpose (as a given task) or in a certain environment (such as ecological conditions).

Let us have a very simplified look at the dynamics of the evolutionary process, taking biological evolution as an example. Mutation comes about through genetic copying mistakes. The new type created through mutation is called a mutant. The purpose of a living being is to create more creatures of its type. If a mutation has the effect that the new mutant can fulfil this purpose better than the already existing type in a certain environment, one can expect the relative percentage of the new type to increase in the population; that is, the frequency of the new type rises. One can call biological 'fitness' the relative number of descendants with which a type is represented in the next generation.[16] However, the definition of 'fitness' seems to be rather controversial among biologists.[17] Important is that 'fitness' has nothing to do with the strength or the survival of any individual whatsoever. 'Fitness' is not a measurable attribute of an individual. It is a statistical value attached to the reproduction probability of an individual of a certain type, relative to a certain ecological environment. 'The fitness W_A [of a certain type A] ... can be defined for a particular environment only.'[18] Under certain circumstances, severe short-sightedness, for example, increases the biological fitness of men, as it results in them not being drafted for military service.[19]

Leaving behind these general characterisations, we will turn to those cultural objects which I have called phenomena of the third kind, especially language, to see if and in what way they fulfil the above conditions.

Condition 1: Language evolution is definitely not teleological. There is no definite preset goal that has to be achieved, something which has been made sufficiently clear in the discussion of the finality thesis (see section 4.3). This is one of the reasons why language evolution cannot be predicted. Language development is, however, partially directed (see section 5.1). It is therefore possible to make trend extrapolations in some domains.

Condition 2: Language evolution is definitely a cumulative process. Being a cumulative process is precisely the criterion that makes something a phenomenon of the third kind. This, too, has been sufficiently discussed (see sections 4.1, 4.2).

Condition 3: In this case the situation is less clear. In linguistic literature one can often find remarks to the effect that language, too, is governed by the mechanism of variation and selection; an example is the aforementioned passage by Max Müller, written in 1870: 'A struggle for life is constantly going on amongst the words and grammatical forms in each language. The better, the shorter, the easier forms are constantly gaining the upper hand, and they owe their success to their own inherent virtue.'[20] In 1880, Hermann Paul wrote in his *Principles of the History of Language*: 'For the rest, purpose plays in the development of language no other part than that assigned to it by Darwin in the development of organic nature, – the greater or lesser fitness of the forms which arise is decisive for their survival or disappearance.'[21]

The well-known contemporary biologist and specialist in the theory of evolution, Richard Dawkins, thinks that 'languages clearly evolve'.[22] In his book *The Selfish Gene*, he stretched the analogy between biological and cultural evolution to its extreme, inventing a new equivalent for the gene (presumably not to be taken too seriously) in the domain of culture: the meme. Memes are, like genes, replicators with high copying-fidelity: 'Copying-fidelity is another way of saying longevity-in-the-form-of-copies.'[23] Memes are units of memory, one might say, just big enough to be transferable *en bloc* from one memory to the next. 'Examples of memes are tunes, ideas, catch-phrases, clothes fashions, ways of making pots or of building arches.'[24] Linguistic units, such as words or idioms, the way to articulate something or how to form a plural, are memes too, of course.

Just as genes propagate themselves in the gene pool by leaping from body to body via sperms or eggs, so memes propagate themselves in the meme pool by leaping from brain to brain via a process which, in the broad sense, can be called imitation.[25]

Just like genes, some memes join up to form co-adapted meme complexes in order to increase their survival value, or infective value. The meme 'God' and the meme 'purgatory' would each by itself never have been as successful as they were, had they not joined forces and built a meme complex together with the meme 'faith'.[26] Memes compete with each other: for scarce storage space, for example. As with genes, 'some memes are more successful in the meme pool than others. This is the analogue of natural selection'.[27] 'Whenever conditions arise in which a new kind of replicator *can* make copies of itself, the new replicators *will* tend to take over, and start a new kind of evolution of their own.'[28]

I would like to break off the presentation of Dawkins's play with analogies at this point and spin it out myself, making it language-specific. However, one thing should be noted in advance. Max Müller's words and forms which 'struggle for survival' and Richard Dawkins's memes which compete for higher frequency in the meme pool have one thing in common: they become active.

We will let our imagination play further. Analogous to the gene pool (the set of genes of an entire population), one can imagine a linguistic meme pool. This would be the set of all linguistic memes in a linguistic community: all linguistic units that are just big enough to be able to travel from one individual competence to another. We are dealing here with a kind of infection.[29] One is infected by use and adoption, that is, learning. In contrast to genes, which stay in the body for life, linguistic memes can 'leave' the competence again through forgetting. Genes have alleles. Where there is a gene for blue eyes, there cannot be one for brown ones. Alleles are rivals competing for a certain place on a chromosome. Linguistic memes have alleles, too. They are rivals competing for a 'place' in speech, alternative expressions which have the same function. I can, for example, express the relationship of possession between my sister and her bicycle in at least three ways: *my sister's bicycle*; *the bicycle of my sister*; *the bicycle that belongs to my sister.* These three alleles compete for a 'place' in my utterances that are expressions of the possessive function. Grammatical forms (*schemata* vs *schemas*) or variants in pronunciation (*advertisement* [ædvə:t smənt] vs [ædvətəismənt]) compete, too, and are therefore alleles. Synonyms are alleles *par excellence*.

Dawkins's analogy seems to have one snag, however: his 'self-replicating memes' are unrealistically active. If he wanted to, he could trace this opinion back to a famous predecessor. 'A transmittable idea constitutes an autonomous entity . . . capable of preserving itself, of growing, of gaining in complexity; and is therefore the object of a selective process', writes Jacques Monod.[30] This is a modern form of cultural vitalism. Genes really do something. They come together to form bodies (plants, animals, and humans), using them for their replication. A gene 'wants' nothing but to be represented as often as possible in the gene pool. It achieves this by contributing to the creation of a body which should, if possible, be fitter than other bodies not containing this gene. A 'good gene' is one that can produce 'efficient survival machines – bodies'.[31]

Memes, however, do not use their brains to replicate themselves. In this analogy, the relation between producer and product has been turned upside down. We are the products of our genes, but the producers of our memes. To this one could object: but not of all of them! We have got almost everything we have in our heads from other people. This is a valid objection. It is even correct to say that I cannot protect myself against the 'intrusion' of a meme. To this extent, the metaphor of infection works as well. I know words or theories that I never intended to learn. But those intruders do not force me to contribute to their multiplication. Nothing in nature corresponds to the distinction between active and passive knowledge. A linguistic meme does not use the human being to increase its success in reproducing itself (as genes do); on the contrary, humans use linguistic memes to increase their success in communication; or, in more general terms, their social success.

What is a good linguistic meme? This question cannot be answered as smoothly as the one concerning a good gene, for two reasons, the first of them being the active–passive asymmetry. It can be very useful to me to know linguistic forms which I would never use myself; even those whose use I detest. Ability to understand more is better than understanding less. From this point of view, my linguistic competence can never be great enough. For its owner, every meme is a good meme. Things are different for the user, which brings us to the second reason: good linguistic memes are those whose use contributes to the success I want to achieve in my communicative actions. Perceptions of success can differ greatly, as we saw in section 4.5. For the gene, high frequency alone is relevant. This, however, can be just what the speaker does not want from a linguistic unit. Social success can sometimes depend upon the degree of linguistic eccentricity. In thinking that some memes are 'more successful in the meme pool than others' and that 'this is the analogue of natural selection', Dawkins is oversimplifying things, at least as far as linguistic evolution is concerned.

The selection mechanism has two levels, which constitute a feedback loop. To present this mechanism I have to go further afield.

Every human being capable of speaking a language has a certain competence. I do not mean an idealised one, called upon by linguists when they wish to refer to the object of a grammar, but an actual existing one. I would like to call it individual competence, as I have before. One of its constituents is Chomsky's I-grammar, but this is only one among many others: strategies, maxims, but most importantly, hypotheses about the individual competences of others. This means expectations about behaviour and expectations about expectations, as we have seen in the context of the Humboldt maxim. There are no two individual competences that are identical. It can be assumed, for example, that there are no two human beings who have exactly the same lexicon at their disposal.[32] Our competence is not fashioned in such a way that, for a given communicative goal, we just call up a certain instrument, suitable for all types of addressees and for all situations. A well-known tyre manufacturer once advertised with something like the following slogan: 'There is no tyre for every weather, but for every weather there is a tyre.' This applies equally well to our linguistic competence: there is no one linguistic instrument for every situation, but for every situation there is an instrument, provided the competence is rich enough.

The individual competence of a human being has the character of a hypothesis. My competence is my hypothesis about how, in a given situation, I can make my addressees believe what I want them to believe, do what I want them to do, or feel what I want them to feel.

It is well known that most speakers do not have any theoretical knowledge of their language. We are, for example, unable to spell out the rules for the use of expressions which we use day in and day out. (If you were asked to provide the rules for the use of the word *head*, you would presumably forget that you cannot say *I have a nose on my head*, but that you can say *I have ears on my head*.) The asymmetry inherent in our linguistic knowledge is a direct result of its hypothetical character. We are unable, so to speak, to 'read our hypotheses backwards'. We can offer a hypothesis for every given situation of language use about which linguistic instrument is the appropriate one that would presumably work, but we cannot offer a hypothesis about a given linguistic instrument and say in which situations it could be used appropriately.

Our individual competence is a problem-orientated hypothesis; it is not a rule-orientated one. (To derive the latter from the former is one of the tasks of a linguist.)

From the hypothetical character of my individual competence follows the experimental character of all my communicative enterprises. Every time I establish communicative contact with someone, I engage in a small social experiment. As we saw in section 4.5, we normally pursue several goals at once when we communicate, of which being understood is only one. To achieve all goals, many factors have to be right. The speaker must correctly assess the situation, the interlocutor, his or her individual competence, background knowledge, and the interlocutor's expectations of the speaker; finally, the speaker has to choose the adequate linguistic tools. It is easy to make mistakes in all these 'calculations'.

We are normally not aware that we are constantly executing small experiments in our everyday acts of communication. This is because they mostly end in success, since our individual competence is a good hypothesis, well-tested in these everyday situations. But there are situations in which we are very much aware of the risks of partial or complete failure: when we are in an interview, when we address a member of the opposite sex in a pub, when we want to sell something, or when we use a foreign language.

Incidentally, the thesis that the individual competence has the character of a hypothesis and its use the character of an experiment does not imply, of course, that one has to adopt a learning theory of language acquisition. This thesis does not say anything about how much of the hypothesis is phylogenetically acquired, and thus ontogenetically given, and how much is ontogenetically acquired.

Successful experiments confirm the hypothesis; those that partially or totally fail lead clever experimenters to modifications of their hypotheses. And so we return to the problem of the variation-and-selection mechanism in language.

Two questions of fundamental importance should be asked: one concerning the level of selection, the other concerning the basis of selection.

Biologists do not readily agree on which level selection takes place, on that of the gene, the individual, the group, or the species. In my opinion, in the case of linguistic evolution, one can choose between two levels: the level of the individual or the level of the linguistic unit. (Nowadays one can safely disregard Schleicher's opinion that languages or even language-families fight with each other for survival and that the Indo-European languages – naturally – win the victory because of certain selection criteria.)

There seems to be more agreement among the biologists concerning the basis of selection. In biology one generally distinguishes (using different terminologies) between two types of selection according to their source of selection: phenotypical selection (also called 'survival selection') and genotypical selection (also called 'reproductive selection').[33] In the case of phenotypical selection, the environment is the basis for selection; it brings about adaptation to certain ecological conditions. In the case of the genotypical selection the basis is sexual partners. The two selection mechanisms can have tendencies that run counter to each other. A stag would presumably sometimes be better equipped for its life in the woods without its protruding antlers. But be this as it may, an antler-less stag would get no chance to transmit its well-adapted shape to its offspring.

One can find analogous selection types in human culture. (Stiletto heels seem to owe their existence solely to the anticipation of reproductive selection.) But I cannot see any reason why one should distinguish between these two types when dealing with linguistic evolution.

One should, instead, distinguish between two other types of selection. One of them is externally motivated, and the other is carried out by the speaker himself. They concern different levels of selection, but they are linked.[34]

I would like to call externally motivated selection 'social selection' and that which is internally motivated 'linguistic selection'. Social selection concerns the person; linguistic selection concerns linguistic units. The two have a feedback relationship.

Let us analyse an example: Tony applies in writing for an internship with Mr Smith. Tony will try to phrase his application as well as he can. He knows that quite a lot depends on the linguistic form of his letter of application. He will make an effort to choose his linguistic means so that Mr Smith gets the impression that Tony is the most suitable candidate. That is to say, Tony will anticipate the expected social selection and, on the basis of this anticipation, select his linguistic means from among those which he expects will be successful in forming his individual competence. This is a communicative experiment.

Suppose the experiment fails; Tony does not get the job. If he is a clever experimenter he will read his application again in the light of this bad news. He cannot expect to get any help from Mr Smith. His negative reply concerns the person, not the linguistic means, but language is generally regarded as part of the person. The diagnosis of Tony's failure is not included in the negative reply. Tony has to make this diagnosis himself and engage in a new experiment, modified in the light of the first.

There is a continuous spiral of selection from which we cannot escape: linguistic selection – social selection – diagnosis – linguistic selection – etc. The reason this process is so full of risks is, first, because we never know whether the ecological conditions will be sufficiently similar the next time, and second, because we can never be sure that our diagnoses are right. Even if my addressee made the diagnosis, I cannot be sure, because he could be mistaken, too.

But there is another feedback channel which is larger and more indirect: Tony's contribution to the invisible-hand process! Even Tony contributes his bit to the upholding and modification of existing conventions through his letter of application. It might be that Tony broke some conventions which Mr Smith regarded as absolutely crucial, and therefore Tony did not get the job. If, however, his transgression was not excessively idiosyncratic and normally tolerated in spoken language, it has perhaps contributed to an invisible-hand process, the end-result of which is a new convention. In this way we are perpetually collaborating in the establishment of norms – norms which later may even cause our failure.

6.2 RESUMÉ AND PLEA FOR EXPLANATORY ADEQUACY

In this book the attempt is made to supplement the history of language with 'a *science, which occupies itself with the general conditions of the existence of the object historically developing*'.[35] A cosmology of language is the condition of possibility for an explanatory historiography of language.

My goal in writing this text was to sketch a picture of language in which its 'continuous change'[36] was nothing external (not just a superimposed fact). This does not imply, however, the much stronger claim that continuous change is an essential or necessary attribute of natural languages (see section 1.2). This claim would mean that natural languages have at least one attribute (or a combination of attributes) from which their continuous change follows with logical necessity. I know of no such attribute. It has been demonstrated that language *use* has certain attributes from which the continuous change of our language follows of necessity (see section 5.1). The claim that these attributes are based on essential features of the human species would need to be substantiated.

'The stream of language flows without interruption',[37] wrote Saussure. But he had difficulties proving the necessity. 'But what supports the necessity for change?',[38] he asked, and answered helplessly: 'Time changes all things; there is no reason why language should escape this universal law.'[39]

Although we might have to leave this question unanswered for lack of sufficient arguments, it is a fact that language change is actually taking place in all natural languages at all times. As we cannot find a counterexample, it is tempting to take this hypothesis as a fact. If we want to understand this fact, we have to develop a concept of language that can cope with it and does not regard it as outside the limits of its theory; an example of this latter view is Chomsky's conception of language and linguistics (see section 5.3), which does not even allow us to ask meaningfully about language change. Classical structuralism, too, has to consider language change as something external, as a disturbance of the system. Whoever regards language exclusively as a system of symbols which reflects the world and can be used to exchange ideas or thoughts will be inclined to see change in language mainly as a mechanism that helps to clear up internal weaknesses of the system (as in the case of the frequently mentioned conflict between homonyms), or as a mechanism used to adapt the depiction, 'language', to the original, the 'world', in case the original has evolved away from its depiction.

We have seen (sections 1.1, 5.1) that, in fact, changes in the world are neither necessary nor sufficient to trigger changes in language. Language change is rather the necessary consequence of the use we make of it (leaving aside, however, the question of whether the way we use language is itself a necessary consequence of human nature).

One of the fundamental theses put forward in this book is that a natural language is above all an instrument or device for exerting influence upon others. This means that communication is a species-specific method that allows us to make someone else do a certain thing. Those who agree to look at language from this point of view will recognise at once that, in the use of this 'method', strategies, success, and failure play a role, and hypotheses concerning the suitability of partners, goals, and situations are relevant; these are concepts that all stress the dynamics of the instrument used in this 'method of influencing'.

This idea was developed, taking a fictitious scenario of the origin of language as a starting point (section 2.1): the fairy tale about the ape-man Charlie and his comrades (a story which owes much to Bruno Strecker's 'little-world people'). This story was also used to illustrate an important aspect of the nature of language and the adequate model of explanation for that aspect. Language is conceived as a 'custom of influence' which emerges 'invisible-handedly' as a phenomenon of the third kind, without a plan or the intention to create it, through the natural behaviour patterns of humans, according to the 'known principles of human nature',[40] as Dugald Stewart would have put it.

The thesis that a so-called natural language is a phenomenon of the third kind, and that an explanation by the invisible hand constitutes the sole mode of explanation suitable for this type of phenomenon, constitutes a central claim made in this book. This thesis transcends a concept of language: it is impossible to understand what culture is and what the central aspects of sociocultural phenomena are if we do not regard them as phenomena of the third kind. The corollary to our central thesis is therefore that language change is a special case of sociocultural change.

It is not my intention to make a bid for theoretical hegemony. I do not deny that a language is (also) a system of symbols, a code, an object of Popper's World 3, Humboldt's *energeia*, or that it can be meaningfully studied as a Chomskian I-grammar. My thesis does not have the form, 'language is not this, but rather that'. It is basically naive to ask what language 'really' is. The issue is not what language 'is', but how one should conceive of it if one is interested in solving certain problems.

Knowing the history of a problem deepens one's insight into the nature of that problem. In Chapters 1–3 the problem was presented with numerous references to the history of language study. In doing so I consciously tried to avoid making a clean cut between a systematic and a historiographical section. My goal was not to write an (even partially) historiographical treatise, but to establish a relationship between the problem of genesis and change and the change and genesis of that problem. The questions concerning the 'life' and 'growth' of language, which so preoccupied nineteenth-century linguists, were never solved. They just disappeared, following the change of paradigm initiated by Saussure, because other questions were regarded as more urgent. As soon as the metaphors of the organism were abandoned in the description of language, the interest in the 'life' of language disappeared as well.

I therefore set myself to the task of beginning where this tradition had left off, taking up the problems which were raised mainly by German linguists at the end of the nineteenth century, and in which they became thoroughly entangled (see section 3.2). To solve these problems, ideas were used which had been put forward mainly by eighteenth-century Scottish philosophers of language and society.

In Chapters 1–3 the historical and systematic evolution of the problem and its solution were presented; in Chapters 4–6 a theory was offered which claims to solve the problem: the theory of phenomena of the third kind, and the explanatory mode of the invisible hand which pertains to them.

Criticism has been voiced against this theory or parts of it on several occasions. I have replied to it elsewhere[41] and do not intend to repeat myself here. However, I would like to examine one objection more closely.

The theory put forward in this book claims that the invisible-hand explanation is the only way language change can be explained. This claim may indeed appear to be unnecessarily intolerant and dogmatic. However, it follows directly from the conception of language presented here, and no other form of explanation is known to exist. In his book *On Explaining Language Change*, Roger Lass put forth good – in my view – arguments, showing that the explanations offered so far in linguistics turn out to be pseudo-explanations, devoid of explanatory power. 'The supposed explanations reduce either to taxonomic or descriptive schemata (which, whatever their merits – and they are considerable . . . – are surely not explanations), or to rather desperate and logically flawed pseudo-arguments.'[42]

Whoever believes that there is any other explanatory mode for phenomena of language change (with the exception of the few examples of authoritative language regulations, such as official terminologies, the reform of orthography, or renamings such as

Reichsbahn (imperial railway) > *Bundesbahn* (federal railway)) would have to show that Lass's arguments are invalid, or present another mode of explanation and prove that it provides valid explanations. One could imagine, however, still another strategy: arguing that the demands made here of an explanation (section 4.2) are unreasonably rigid. One could plead for a weaker concept of explanation, show that it, too, has (some) explanatory power, and claim that such a concept of explanation is suitable for linguistics. This is the strategy that Rudolf Windisch seems to have opted for. Challenging Roger Lass, he pleads for a type of explanation which he calls '"correct" linguistic explanation'.[43] (He does not explain why he puts 'correct' in inverted commas throughout.) A '"correct" linguistic explanation' should apparently mention the following:

(a) language-internal reasons (e.g., functionalistic schemata of explanation, such as the equilibrium of the system, homonymy, avoidance of homonymy, and so on);
(b) external reasons (substratic–superstratic influence; the prestige of a highly regarded social group, and so on)'.[44]

Windisch chooses as an example (among others) the famous case of a so-called 'flight of homonyms' in Gascognic. In that language, a rooster is called *bigey* (which derives from the Latin *vicarius*) and not *gat*, as one would expect, given the normal pattern of sound change from Latin to Gascognic. The reason is – such is the 'explanation' – that the sound change from Latin to Gascognic was such that both Latin *cattus* (cat) and *gallus* (rooster) had to become *gat* in Gascognic.

This is the 'classic' pattern of explanation which one could call 'hymonym flight because of homonyms conflict', and to which all the objections apply which have been put forward in section 4.3 for the *englisch* homonymy, as well as all those put forward by Roger Lass in his section 3.5.

Windisch comments as follows on the pattern of the '"correct" explanation':

It goes without saying that 'correct' explanations (which can only be recognised as such by their plausibility in a kind of circular argument) suffer from one fundamental defect: they are indeed only partially applicable, or to put it in paradoxical terms, they are only valid where they apply, as for example an explanation (or 'principle' of explanation or 'thesis') of a homonymy (that should be avoided), such as the clash between Lat. *gallus* and *cattus* as '*gat*' 'cat' (sic!) in Gascognic through regular sound change. . . . One would surely not expect to find a similar 'homophonie gênante' every time that such a (theoretically possible) sound change occurred. In the special case of southwestern French it must, however, be regarded as the 'correct' explanation.[45]

I do not want to comment on the specific problems of this passage, and so will say only a few words on the structure of the argument.

So-called explanations which are 'only valid where they apply', as Windisch puts it in wonderfully simple terms, are not called 'explanations'. Windisch should not have put the word *correct* in quotation marks, but rather the word *explanation*. It is not so much the correctness of the description that is doubtful, but its explanatory power, its status as an explanation. The so-called 'explanatory "principle"' (I do not quite see the function of the quotation marks here either) – '"homophonie gênante" is brought under control by the therapeutic measure of replacing one of the homophones' – is analytic and therefore null and void as an argument. As the existence of homophony (homonymy) is neither necessary nor sufficient to explain the substitution of one word by another, something that Windisch concedes, 'homophonie gênante' exists per definition precisely when so-called homonym flight has taken place. His argument is a case of the classic *post hoc, ergo propter hoc* fallacy. Or, in Lass's words:

'Logically, this seems to be of the form:
(a) p ⊃ q
(b)   q
(c) ∴ p

That is, it is an instance of the fallacy of affirming the consequence.'[46]

Since Windisch presents his theses as a reply to those of Lass, one would expect either an explanation as to why this fallacy does not disturb him or an argument that there is no such fallacy. The latter could be demonstrated by defining *homophonie gênante* without resorting to the substitution of a non-homophonous word of equivalent meaning for one of the two homophones, and then demonstrating with examples that *homophonie gênante* exists or existed without any such therapeutic substitution.

Change and stasis of a language cannot be understood without a *Prinzipienwissenschaft*, as Hermann Paul called it, or a cosmology, as it is sometimes called today (though somewhat bombastically). 'The existence of the structures with which the theory of complex phenomena is concerned can be made intelligible only by what the physicists would call a cosmology',[47] writes von Hayek, in the footsteps of Paul: 'The effectual scrutiny of the conditions of historical growth, taken in conjunction with general logic, gives at the same time the basis for the doctrine of method.'[48]

This certainly does not mean, of course, that one can explain all and everything with such a 'cosmology'. Assuming this would confuse necessary and sufficient conditions. Why p, t, and k, for example, were affected by the sound shift, 'whereas l, r, m and n escaped unscathed', is a question asked by Peter Eyer,[49] assuming perhaps that my inability to provide an explanation for this fact constitutes an argument against my theory. Now, I do not know the answer to this, and it is doubtful that it will ever be known. To be explainable, a fact in the history of a language has to be at a suitable distance from the explanatory basis. To demonstrate what this means, I shall use a simple example of arithmetic taken from Hans-Jürgen Heringer.

Let us look at a statement that can be found in any history of language: '$p > f$. It is supposed to mean that 'A p in Indo-European corresponds to an f in Germanic', a fact which constitutes part of the so-called Germanic sound shift. An explanation of this fact would consist in showing which maxims led under which circumstances to actions, whose consequence it would be that 'now' an f-sound is articulated where a p-sound had been articulated 'before'. In a 'thought-experiment', Heringer calculates what would be the real 'empirical' basis of such a statement: 'Such innocent looking statements are about highly complex processes, and therefore common historiography of language suffers from serious macroscopy.'[50] Following Heringer[51] to take a closer look at this macroscopy, we will assume that this evolution spans about two centuries, and furthermore, that about 100 million Teutons have participated in this process, communicating verbally with each other daily for about an hour, pronouncing an average of 2,000 words of five phonemes in length. That means 10^8 speakers produced 10^4 sound events over a period of 7×10^4 days; the result is 7×10^{16} sound productions. Leaving aside for the moment the fact that, for sound changes to occur, the reception by the addressee is at least as important as the contribution by the speaker, this rough calculation shows that '$p > f$' means approximately the following: at the point where at time t_1 p-sounds were articulated, 70,000,000,000,000,000 sound events later, f-sounds were articulated. 'I hope that this *Gedankenexperiment* may convince us that statements such as ($p > f$) belong to a very specific kind of empiricism.'[52]

What can we learn from this number game? There are historiographic statements which are legitimately descriptive, but which simply cannot be made candidates for explanatory effort in any meaningful way. In order to explain phenomena in language's history, an appropriate dimension must be chosen. This can only be on a structural level that correlates meaningfully with the level of linguistic action.

Whoever wants to know how the amoeba developed into the elephant will have to be content with a very general answer, a so-called explanation in principle. But even where the scope of analysis is right, we cannot always reach an explanation, because we lack the necessary facts – facts that possibly no one will ever know. Because the historiography of language has regarded itself up to now as an essentially descriptive and not explanatory type of history (according to its own claims), the necessary data are just not available. Finally, it is to be assumed that in language change, especially phonological change, there exist chance events which, by definition, cannot be explained.

Nevertheless, the claim made by Chomsky twenty-five years ago for a theory of grammar is the same for a historical theory: 'Although even descriptive adequacy on a large scale is by no means easy to approach, it is crucial for the productive development of linguistic theory that much higher goals than this be pursued.'[53] The goal is explanatory adequacy.

A theory of the history of language has explanatory adequacy in so far as it succeeds in correlating reconstructed historical data with descriptive adequacy to the linguistic actions whose consequences they are; that is to say, by demonstrating that they are the necessary and unintended consequences of individual actions carried out according to specific maxims of action under specific ecological circumstances.

I believe to have shown that this claim can, in principle, be substantiated, although in many cases the contingent deficits in our knowledge may prevent it.

Notes

1 THE PROBLEM OF LANGUAGE CHANGE

1 Strehlow 1907–15, p. 55, quoted from Boretzky 1981, p. 75.
2 Austen 1813b/1923, pp. 170ff.
3 Austen 1816a/1923, p. 189; Austen 1813a/1923, p. 318: 'on the catch' meaning 'with the wish to marry'; 'nuncheon' meaning 'a 'liquid' snack between meals'.
4 Austen 1818/1923, p. 107.
5 Austen 1816b/1923, p. 200.
6 Fleischer 1971, p. 9.
7 Stam 1976, p. 1.
8 Paul 1910, p. 369.
9 This has been demonstrated by David Lewis (1969, p. 70) in particular.
10 See Wildgen 1985.
11 Lorenz 1973, p. 47.
12 Toulmin 1972, p. 331, note 1.
13 Cf. L. Weisgerber 1971, p. 9; de Saussure 1916/1974, pp. 6, 93.
14 Schleicher 1863/1869, pp. 20ff.
15 Cf. Schleicher *ibid.*, p. 62.
16 Grimm 1819/1968, p. 6.
17 Lüdtke 1980, p. 3.
18 Chomsky 1980, p. 11.
19 See Keller 1977a, p. 19.
20 See e.g. Wunderlich 1976, pp. 37f.; Ronneberger-Sibold 1980, pp. 25, 33, 134, 135; Rehbein 1977.
21 Ullmann-Margalit 1978, p. 280.
22 Nickl 1980. I wish to thank Bruno Strecker for drawing my attention to this picture.
23 Cf. von Hayek 1967b.
24 Cf. von Hayek 1956. I owe this bibliographical hint to V. Vanberg.
25 Engels to Joseph Bloch 21 and 22 September 1890 (Marx and Engels 1967, p. 464).

2 HISTORICAL RECONSTRUCTION

1 *Bulletin de la Société de Linguistique de Paris* I (1871), p. iii, quoted from Stam 1976, p. 259.
2 Quoted from Stam 1976, p. 256.
3 Strecker 1987; see also Heringer 1985.
4 Quoted from Aarsleff 1982, pp. 194ff. The question reads in the original: 'En supposant les hommes abandonnés à leurs facultés naturelles, sont-ils en état d'inventer le langage?'
5 Süβmilch 1766, Preface, no page number. Cf. Aarsleff 1982, pp. 187ff.
6 Cf. Wilson 1975, p. 581.
7 Hockett and Altmann 1968.
8 This definition of 'mutual knowledge' is a simplified version. See Keller 1974.
9 'If and only if' is presumably not right, because this way of putting it is probably not satisfactory. It is impossible to provide in this context an exhaustive discussion of Grice's explication of 'utterer's meaning'.
10 See for example Hildebrandt-Nilshon 1980.
11 Quoted from Arens 1969, p. 56.
12 Quoted from Arens 1969, p. 95 (originally in *Miscellania Berolinensia*, Berlin 1710, pp. 1–16).
13 von Hayek 1966, p. 126.
14 After 1704 he dropped the 'de'.
15 See the inventory of his works in Mandeville 1732/1924, vol. I, pp. xxx ff.
16 von Hayek 1966, p. 127.
17 'Journeyman parson' was a slang term for a curate. (Mandeville 1732/1924, p. 30, note 1.)
18 Mandeville 1732/1924, vol. I, p. 385.
19 The first German translation of *The Fable of the Bees* appeared in 1761; *Faust* appeared in 1790.
20 Vanberg 1982, p. 43.
21 Ferguson 1767, p. 204.
22 *Ibid.*, p. 205 (my italics).
23 von Hayek 1966, p. 140.
24 Stewart 1858/1971, p. 33; Peardon 1966, p. 14 ('Read by Mr. Stewart, January 21, and March 18, 1793').
25 Stewart 1858/1971, p. 34. Kittsteiner 1980, pp. 179ff. provides a historical and philosophical analysis of Stewart.
26 Smith 1776/1970, p. 400.

3 IN THE PRISON OF DICHOTOMIES

1 von Hayek 1967b, p. 72 (my italics).
2 Müller 1864, p. 22.
3 Frei 1929, p. 24.
4 von Hayek 1983, p. 170; see also von Hayek 1988, Ch. 1.
5 von Hayek 1983, p. 170.

6 *Ibid.*, p. 166.
7 Wittgenstein 1953, section 219.
8 Cicero had already pointed this out: *Consuetudo est quasi altera natura.*
9 von Hayek 1983, p. 165.
10 See the discussion in Beeh 1981, pp. 92ff.
11 See *ibid.*, p. 99.
12 Lorenz 1965, p. 44.
13 Beeh 1981, pp. 94ff.
14 von Hayek 1983, p. 164.
15 On the theory and evolution of complex societies, see Corning 1983.
16 von Hayek 1983, p. 165.
17 von Hayek 1966, p. 129.
18 Schleicher 1868, p. 206.
19 Schleicher 1863/1869, pp. 20ff.
20 *Ibid.*, p. 25.
21 *Ibid.*, pp. 19ff.
22 Whitney 1873, pp. 208–9.
23 Scherer 1874, p. 412.
24 Schleicher 1863/1869, p. 26.
25 *Ibid.*, p. 28.
26 See Keller 1983, p. 34.
27 Schleicher 1863/1869, p. 55.
28 *Ibid.*, pp. 33ff.
29 *Ibid.*, p. 21.
30 Müller 1864, p. 42.
31 *Ibid.*, p. 22.
32 *Ibid.*
33 *Ibid.*, p. 31.
34 *Ibid.*, p. 35.
35 *Ibid.*, p. 29.
36 *Ibid.*, p. 38 (my italics).
37 Spencer 1864/1966, p. 432 (my italics); see also Part II, Ch. II: 'Development'.
38 Müller 1864, p. 38.
39 Whitney uses this term on p. 50 of *Language and the Study of Language* (1867).
40 Whitney 1867, p. 686 (addition by the German translator of *Language and the Study of Language*, Julius Jolly).
41 Whitney 1875, p. 266.
42 Whitney 1873, p. 301.
43 *Ibid.*, pp. 301ff.
44 *Ibid.*, p. 316.
45 Müller 1864, p. 41 (my italics).
46 Whitney 1873, p. 355. (Darwin, too, points out this passage; see Darwin 1871/1901, p. 131, note 53.)
47 Chomsky 1980, p. 10.
48 Chomsky 1982, p. 107.

49 Chomsky 1980, p. 11.
50 Whitney 1873, p. 301.
51 '&' stands for 'as well as'; '/' stands for 'one of the two but not both'; '⊃' stands for 'implies'; '-' stands for 'not'.
52 Ferguson 1767, p. 205.

4 THE WORKING OF THE INVISIBLE HAND

1 Haakonssen 1981, p. 24. I would like to thank von Hayek for this bibliographical hint.
2 There are different terminologies available. I shall use the one I introduced in Keller 1977a.
3 See *ibid.*, p. 19.
4 See Coseriu 1958/1973, pp. 29f, pp. 112ff.; Cherubim 1983, p. 9; Ronneberger-Sibold 1980, p. 37.
5 Müller 1864, p. 41.
6 Whitney 1873, p. 355.
7 Menger 1883/1963, p. 146.
8 *Ibid.*
9 *Ibid.*, pp. 146ff.
10 *Ibid.*, p. 147.
11 *Ibid.*, p. 148.
12 *Ibid.*
13 *Ibid.*, p. 149.
14 *Ibid.*, p. 158.
15 *Ibid.*, p. 150.
16 Smith 1776/1970, p. 400.
17 See Cropsey 1979 and Ullmann-Margalit 1978, p. 287.
18 Nozick 1974, p. 18.
19 *Ibid.*, p. 19.
20 Hempel 1965, p. 447.
21 See Wimmer 1983.
22 See Köhler and Altmann 1986, p. 254.
23 Ullmann-Margalit 1978, p. 267.
24 For a theory of 'residential segregation', see Schelling 1969.
25 It goes without saying that racial motives also underlie the 'organic' growth of ghettos, but they have different effects than in this case.
26 Lass 1980, p. 9.
27 See Keller 1989.
28 See Ullmann-Margalit 1978, p. 271.
29 Nozick 1974, p. 18.
30 Rádl 1909, pp. 125ff.
31 Graham 1975, p. 61.
32 On the topic of inflation in the domain of culture see Gombrich 1979, Ch. II.
33 Strawson 1971, p. 189.
34 Mauthner 1912/1982, pp. 93ff.

35 See section 3.2.
36 See section 3.2.
37 de Saussure 1916/1974, p. 77.
38 Ayren 1986, p. 110.
39 Coseriu 1958/1973, p. 178.
40 See Grewendorf, Hamm, and Sternefeld 1987, pp. 22ff; see section 5.3.
41 Coseriu 1958/1973, p. 193f; see also Coseriu 1983.
42 Coseriu 1980, p. 143.
43 Coseriu 1958/1973, p. 182.
44 Coseriu 1980, p. 142.
45 Coseriu 1958, pp. 198ff.
46 A finalistic explanation is an intentional explanation pointing forwards; it provides an answer to the question *what for*. The *why*-question is not necessarily a question about the causes; it may be a question about the reasons. An answer to the question about reasons is equally an intentional explanation, an intentional explanation pointing backwards.
47 Cf. Grimm's dictionary.
48 See section 4.2.
49 Coseriu 1958/1973, pp. 193ff.
50 Ronneberger-Sibold 1980, p. 37.
51 Osche 1987, p. 509.
52 See section 2.1.
53 See section 2.1.
54 This only appears to be a circular claim. In saying how something functions, one does not say which function it has.
55 Ullmann-Margalit 1978, p. 279.
56 Fanselow and Felix 1987, p. 93.
57 See section 4.2.
58 Lass 1980, p. 82.
59 Humboldt 1836/1988, p. 115.
60 Grice 1975.
61 Coseriu 1958/1973, p. 196.
62 Lüdtke 1980, p. 4.
63 Alarcos Llorach 1968, p. 117.
64 Lass 1980, p. 136.
65 Cf. Watzlawick, Beavin, and Jackson 1967; on this topic, see Keller 1977a.
66 On the problem of misunderstanding see, for example, Dascal 1985; Dobrick 1985.
67 Lewis 1969, p. 25.
68 Humboldt 1836/1988, p. 50.
69 Levin 1988.
70 We are dealing here with a cellular automaton; on this issue see Silbar 1987.
71 Levin 1988, p. 4.
72 Using a very similar model, T.C. Schelling (1969) has tried to explain the emergence of ghettos in his article 'Models of Segregation'. It is immediately clear that, for example, the maxim of a tenant 'Move out

if you belong to a minority in your neighbourhood' leads to analogous distributions. Ullmann-Margalit (1978) mentions Schelling's model as an example of an invisible-hand explanation.
73 Levin 1988, pp. 6ff.
74 Lüdtke 1980.
75 On originality as a possible maxim, see Lüdtke 1986.
76 See Radnitzky 1983, p. 84.
77 Martinet 1960, p. 18.

5 DISCUSSION

1   Lüdtke 1980, p. 10.
2   *Ibid.*, p. 15.
3   Lass 1980, p. 3.
4   Lüdtke 1986, p. 6.
5   Lüdtke p.c.
6   Lüdtke p.c.
7   Sapir 1921, Ch. VII.
8   *Ibid.*, p. 155.
9   Lass 1987, p. 186.
10 Aitchison 1987, pp. 16f.
11 *Ibid.*, p. 16.
12 Cf. Bates 1984.
13 The third principle concerns the psychology of perception. It may be that the principle of economy, too, plays a role in the segmentation of the world into units, since it is supposedly economical to keep down the number of categories.
14 Aitchison 1987, pp. 29f.
15 Bailey 1980, p. 175.
16 Lass 1980, p. 43.
17 Wurzel 1992, p. 225.
18 *Ibid.*, p. 226.
19 *Ibid.*
20 *Ibid.*, p. 226.
21 Wurzel 1989, p. 11.
22 *Ibid.*, p. 75.
23 Wurzel 1992, p. 227.
24 Wurzel 1989, p. 21.
25 Wurzel 1992, p. 229.
26 *Ibid.*
27 Mayerthaler 1981, p. 2.
28 Wurzel 1988, p. 490.
29 *Ibid.*
30 Stein 1990, p. 289.
31 Stein 1988, p. 474.
32 Stein 1990, p. 286.
33 Lass 1980, p. 18.

34 *Ibid.*, p. 19.
35 *Ibid.*
36 Cf. Albert 1990.
37 Cf. Slote 1989.
38 Cf. Lyons 1968, pp. 89f.
39 Grimm 1819/1968, p. 2.
40 See Jäger 1984, pp. 711f.
41 *Ibid.*
42 Coseriu 1958/1973, p. 27.
43 On the question of reconstruction, see Jäger 1976 and Scheerer 1980.
44 de Saussure 1916/1974, p. 140.
45 Garaudy 1973, p. 139.
46 Coseriu 1980, p. 144.
47 *Ibid.*, p. 136.
48 Menger 1883/1963, p. 150.
49 Coseriu 1958/1973, p. 112.
50 von Hayek 1967b, p. 75.
51 Humboldt 1836/1988, p. 48.
52 *Ibid.*, p. 49.
53 Coseriu 1958/1973, p. 45.
54 Humboldt 1836/1988, p. 49.
55 Chomsky 1986, p. 3.
56 Chomsky 1986, esp. section 2.3, pp. 21ff. I assume that this distinction
    has its origin in Cloak 1975. In his essay 'Is Cultural Ethology Possible?'
    Cloak distinguishes between 'I-culture' and 'M(aterialized)-culture'.
    But unlike Chomsky he does not consider M-culture as being only of
    heuristic value for the study of I-culture. He recognises that both stand
    in a relation of feedback and have to be considered jointly.
57 Grewendorf, Hamm, and Sternefeld 1987, p. 24.
58 Chomsky 1982, p. 108.
59 Chomsky 1986, p. 26.
60 Chomsky 1982, p. 107.
61 Chomsky 1986, p. 26.
62 *Ibid.*, p. 23.
63 *Ibid.*, p. 27 (my emphasis).
64 Fanselow and Felix 1987, p. 58.
65 *Ibid.*, p. 61.
66 *Ibid.*, p. 62.
67 Frege 1966, p. 115.
68 Fanselow and Felix 1987, p. 62.
69 *Ibid.*, p. 59.
70 *Ibid.*, p. 60.
71 *Ibid.*
72 See Hurford 1987, p. 25.
73 Chomsky 1965, p. 3.
74 Chomsky 1986, p. 17.
75 *Ibid.*
76 Hurford 1987, p. 24.

77 *Ibid.*, p. 26.
78 Chomsky 1980, 1981, p. 80.
79 Grewendorf, Hamm, and Sternefeld 1987, p. 22.
80 Chomsky 1981, p. 8 (my emphasis).
81 Hurford 1987, p. 25.
82 Lass 1980, p. 3; see also p. 130 note 12. As Roger Lass says of himself that 'I'm a bit of a Platonist' (p.c.), he might possibly accept Chomsky's concept of the P(latonic)-language (see Chomsky 1986, p. 33).
83 Lass 1987, p. 170.
84 Popper and Eccles 1977, p. 38.
85 *Ibid.*, p. 16.
86 *Ibid.*
87 *Ibid.*, p. 11.
88 *Ibid.*, p. 38.
89 *Ibid.*, p. 16.
90 *Ibid.*, p. 40.
91 I am not sure if being part of reality can be called an attribute of an object.
92 Popper and Eccles 1977, pp. 38f.
93 *Ibid.*, p. 450.
94 *Ibid.* (my emphasis).
95 *Ibid.*, p. 10.
96 *Ibid.*, p. 39.
97 *Ibid.*, p. 47.
98 *Ibid.*, p. 48.
99 *Ibid.*, p. 109.
100 *Ibid.*, p. 144.
101 *Ibid.*
102 *Ibid.*
103 *Ibid.*, p. 450.
104 Lass 1984, p. 4.
105 *Ibid.*, pp. 4f. (emphasis by Lass).
106 *Ibid.*, p. 5 (emphasis by Lass).
107 Lass 1987, p. 170.
108 Lass 1984, p. 8.
109 Lass 1987, p. 170.
110 Or, as a borderline case, by many actions of a single person. Erica García (p.c.) objects that World 2, the individual's inner world, is the result of the actions of many as well.

6 CONCLUSION

1 I owe this example to a personal communication from Roger Lass; as well as the tip that the *Satzklammer* is being loosened in German, too. Compare *Ich **habe** schon besseren Wein als diesen **getrunken*** versus colloquially *Ich **habe** schon besseren Wein getrunken als diesen.* (I have drunk better wine than this before.)
2 Maynard Smith 1972, p. 43.

3   Coseriu 1958/1973, p. 181, note 7.
4   *Ibid.*, p. 282.
5   Humboldt 1836/1988, p. 133.
6   *Ibid.*, p. 49.
7   Rádl 1909, p. 128 (emphasis by Rádl).
8   Quoted by von Hayek 1983, p. 172.
9   The first passage was written by a certain Sir Nathaniel Barneby (1904), the second by Rowland Thirlmare (1907); both quoted in Koch 1973, p. 96. On social Darwinism, see also Dobzhansky 1962.
10   von Hayek 1983, p. 173.
11   Max Müller in 'Nature', 6 January 1870, p. 257, quoted from Darwin 1871/1901, p. 138.
12   Schleicher 1863/1869, pp. 64 and 66.
13   Gerard, Kluckhohn, and Rapoport 1956, p. 14.
14   Maynard Smith 1972, pp. 92ff. It must be stressed that not all changes are adaptive, neither in biology nor in linguistics; random effects must be reckoned with. But these are, by definition, unexplainable.
15   Gerard, Kluckhohn, and Rapoport 1956, p. 15.
16   See Cavalli-Sforza 1971, pp. 535ff.
17   See Huxley 1963, p. xviii.
18   Maynard Smith 1972, p. 97.
19   *Ibid.*, p. 84.
20   Max Müller in 'Nature', 6 January 1870, quoted from Darwin 1871/1901, p. 138.
21   Paul 1880/1970, p. 13.
22   Dawkins 1986, p. 217.
23   Dawkins 1976, p. 30.
24   *Ibid.*, p. 206.
25   *Ibid.*
26   *Ibid.*, pp. 212ff.
27   *Ibid.*, p. 208.
28   *Ibid.*
29   Cavalli-Sforza 1971, p. 537.
30   Monod 1969, p. 16, quoted from Toulmin 1972, p. 319.
31   Dawkins 1976, pp. 92ff.
32   Hurford 1987, pp. 27ff.
33   Cf. Huxley 1963, pp. xix ff.
34   Cf. Toulmin 1972, pp. 394ff.
35   Paul 1880/1970, p. xxi (italics by Paul).
36   Paul 1910, p. 369.
37   de Saussure 1916/1974, p. 140.
38   *Ibid.*, p. 76.
39   *Ibid.*, p. 77; see also p. 74.
40   Stewart 1858/1971, p. 34.
41   See Keller 1984, 1987.
42   Lass 1980, p. xi.
43   Windisch 1988, pp. 114, 116.
44   *Ibid.*, p. 116.

45 *Ibid.*, p. 116ff.
46 Lass 1980, pp. 78ff.
47 von Hayek 1967b, p. 76.
48 Paul 1880/1970.
49 Eyer 1983, p. 74.
50 Heringer 1988, p. 3.
51 *Ibid.*, pp. 3ff.
52 *Ibid.*, p. 5.
53 Chomsky 1965, p. 24.

References

When two years are indicated after an author's name, e.g. 'Smith, Adam (1776/1970) *The Wealth of Nations*, vol. I, reprint, London and New York.' the first specifies the date of the original edition and the second that of the edition from which I have quoted.

Aarsleff, Hans (1982) *From Locke to Saussure. Essays on the Study of Language and Intellectual History*, London.

Adamska-Sałaciak, Arleta (1991) 'Language Change as a Phenomenon of the Third Kind', *Folia Linguistica Historica* XII/1–2, 159–80.

Aitchison, Jean (1987) 'The Language Lifegame', in Willem Koopman, Frederike van der Leek, Olga Fischer, and Roger Eaton (eds), *Explanation and Linguistic Change*, Amsterdam, 11–32.

Alarcos Llorach, Emilio (1968) *Fonología española*, 4th augmented and revised edn, Madrid.

Albert, Hans (1990) 'Methodologischer Individualismus und historische Analyse', in Karl Acham and Winfried Schulze (eds), *Teil und Ganzes. Zum Verhältnis von Einzel- und Gesamtanalyse in Geschichts- und Sozialwissenschaften*, Munich, 219–39.

Anttila, Raimo (1992) Review of *Sprachwandel. Von der unsichtbaren Hand in der Sprache*, by Rudi Keller, *Studies in Language* 16/1, 213–18.

Arens, Hans (1969) *Sprachwissenschaft. Der Gang ihrer Entwicklung von der Antike bis zur Gegenwart*, 2nd edn, Freiburg and Munich.

Austen, Jane (1813a/1923) *Sense and Sensibility*, vol. I; (1813b/1923) *Pride and Prejudice*, vol. II; (1816a/1923) *Mansfield Park*, vol. III; (1816b/1923) *Emma*, vol. IV; (1818/1923) *Persuasion*, vol. V. *The Novels of Jane Austen*, ed. R.W. Chapman, 1st edn 1923, London, New York, and Toronto.

Ayren, Armin (1986) 'Wenn wir hätten, was wir haben. Der gestörte Konjunktiv', *Sprach-Störungen. Beiträge zur Sprachkritik*, ed. Hans-Martin Gauger, Munich and Vienna, 110–24.

Bailey, Charles-James N. (1980) 'Old and New Views on Language History and Language Relationships', in Helmut Lüdtke (ed.) *Kommunikationstheoretische Grundlagen des Sprachwandels*, Berlin and New York, 139–81.

Bates, Elizabeth (1984) 'Bioprogrammes and the Innateness Hypothesis', *The Behavioral and Brain Sciences* 7/2, 188–90.

Beeh, Volker (1981) *Sprache und Spracherlernung. Unter mathematisch-biologischer Perspektive*, Berlin and New York.

Boretzky, Norbert (1981) 'Das Indogermanische Sprachwandelmodell und Wandel in exotischen Sprachen', *Zeitschrift für vergleichende Sprachforschung* 95/1, 49–80.

Cavalli-Sforza, Luigi (1971) 'Similarities and Dissimilarities of Sociocultural and Biological Evolution', in F.R. Hodson *et al.* (eds) *Mathematics in Archeological and Historical Sciences*, Edinburgh, 535–41.

Cherubim, Dieter (1983) 'Trampelpfad zum Sprachwandel', *Zeitschrift für Germanistische Linguistik* 11, 65–71.

Chomsky, Noam (1965) *Aspects of the Theory of Syntax*, Cambridge, Mass.

—— (1980) *Rules and Representations*, New York.

—— (1981) *Lectures on Government and Binding*, Dordrecht.

—— (1982) *The Generative Enterprise: A Discussion with Riny Huybregts and Henk van Riemsdijk*, Dordrecht.

—— (1986) *Knowledge of Language. Its Nature, Origin and Use*, New York.

Cloak, F.T.Jr (1975) 'Is Cultural Ethology Possible?' *Human Ecology* 3/3, 161–82.

Corning, Peter E. (1983) *The Synergism Hypothesis. A Theory of Progressive Evolution*, New York.

Coseriu, Eugenio (1958/1973) *Sincronía, diachronía, e historia. El problema del cambio lingüístico*, 2nd revised edn, Madrid.

—— (1980) 'Vom Primat der Geschichte', *Sprachwissenschaft* 5/2, 125–45.

—— (1983) 'Linguistic Change Does not Exist', *Linguistica Nuova ed Antica: Rivista di Linguistica Classica Medioevale e Moderna*, Anno I, 51–63.

Cropsey, Joseph (1979) 'The Invisible Hand: Moral and Political Considerations', in Gerald P. O'Driscoll Jr (ed.) *Adam Smith and Modern Political Economy*, Ames, Iowa, 165–76.

Darwin, Charles (1871/1901) *The Descent of Man and Selection in Relation to Sex*, London.

Dascal, Marcello (1985) 'The Relevance of Misunderstanding', in Thomas T. Ballmer and Roland Posner (eds), *Nach-Chomskysche Linguistik*, Berlin and New York, 194–210.

Dawkins, Richard (1976) *The Selfish Gene*, Oxford.

—— (1986) *The Blind Watchmaker*, New York and London.

Dobrick, Martin (1985) *Gegenseitiges (Miβ-)Verstehen in der dyadischen Kommunikation*, Münster.

Dobzhansky, Theodosius (1962) *Mankind Evolving*, New Haven, Conn.

Dressler, Wolfgang U., Mayerthaler, Willi, Panagl, Oswald, and Wurzel, Wolfgang U. (1987) *Leitmotifs in Natural Morphology*, Amsterdam and Philadelphia.

Eyer, Peter (1983) '"... und trampelt durch die Saaten"', *Zeitschrift für Germanistische Linguistik* 11, 72–7.

Fanselow, Gisbert and Felix, Sascha (1987) *Sprachtheorie. Eine Einführung in die generative Grammatik*, vol. 1, Tübingen.

Ferguson, Adam (1767) *An Essay on the History of Civil Society*, Edinburgh.

Fleischer, Wolfgang (1971) *Wortbildung der deutschen Gegenwartssprache*, 2nd edn, Tübingen.

Frege, Gottlob (1966) 'Über die Zahlen des Herrn H. Schubert', in Günther Patzig (ed.) *Logische Untersuchungen*, Göttingen, 113–38.

Frei, Henri (1929) *La Grammaire des Fautes*, Paris, Geneva and Leipzig.

Garaudy, Roger (1973) *Die Alternative*, Vienna, Munich, and Zurich.

Gerard, R.W., Kluckhohn, Clyde, and Rapoport, Anatol (1956) 'Biological and Cultural Evolution. Some Analogies and Explanations', *Behavioral Science* 1, 6–34.

Gombrich, Ernst H. (1979) *Ideals and Idols*, Oxford.

Graham, Alma (1975) 'The Making of a Nonsexist Dictionary', in Barrie Thorne and Nancy Hemley (eds) *Language and Sex. Difference and Dominance*, Rowley, Mass., 57–63.

Grewendorf, Günther, Hamm, Fritz, and Sternefeld, Wolfgang (1987) *Sprachliches Wissen. Eine Einführung in moderne Theorien der Beschreibung*, Frankfurt-on-Main.

Grice, Herbert Paul (1968) 'Utterer's Meaning, Sentence-Meaning, and World-Meaning', *Foundations of Language* 4, 1–18.

—— (1969) 'Utterer's Meaning and Intentions', *The Philosophical Review* 78, 147–77.

—— (1975) 'Logic and Conversation', in P. Cole and J. Morgan (eds) *Syntax and Semantics*, vol. 3, New York, San Francisco, and London, 41–58.

Grimm, Jakob (1819/1968) *Vorreden zur deutschen Grammatik von 1819 und 1822*, reprint, Darmstadt.

Grimm, Jakob and Grimm, Wilhelm (1862) *Deutsches Wörterbuch*, vol. 3, Leipzig.

Haakonssen, Knud (1981) *The Science of a Legislator. The Jurisprudence of David Hume and Adam Smith*, Cambridge.

Hayek, Friedrich August von (1956) 'Über den "Sinn" sozialer Institutionen', *Schweizer Monatshefte* 36, Zurich, 512–24.

—— (1966) 'Dr Bernard Mandeville', *Proceedings of the British Academy*, LII, 125–41.

—— (1967a) 'The Results of Human Action but not of Human Design', in Friedrich August von Hayek, *Studies in Philosophy, Politics and Economics*, Chicago and Toronto, 96–105.

—— (1967b) 'Notes on the Evolution of Systems of Conduct', in Friedrich August von Hayek, *Studies in Philosophy. Politics and Economics*, Chicago and Toronto, 66–81.

—— (1983) 'Die überschätzte Vernunft', in Rupert J. Riedl and Franz Kreuzer (eds) *Evolution und Menschenbild*, Hamburg, 164–92.

—— (1988) 'The Fatal Conceit. The Errors of Socialism', in W.W. Bartley (ed.), *The Collected Works of Friedrich August Hayek*, vol. III, London and New York.

Hempel, Carl G. (1965) *Aspects of Scientific Explanation and other Essays in the Philosophy of Science*, New York.

Heringer, Hans J. (1985) 'Not by Nature nor by Intention: the Normative Power of Language Signs', in Thomas T. Ballmer (ed.) *Linguistic Dynamics*, Berlin and New York, 251–75.

—— (1988) *An Axiomatics of Language Evolution*, mimeo, Augsburg.

Hildebrandt-Nilshon, Martin (1980) *Die Entwicklung der Sprache. Phylogenese und Ontogenese*, Frankfurt-on-Main and New York.

Hockett, Charles F. and Altmann, S. (1968) 'A Note on Design Features', in T.A. Sebeok (ed.) *Animal Communication*, Bloomington, Ind., 61–72.

Humboldt, Wilhelm von (1836/1988) *On Language. The Diversity of Human Language-Structure and its Influence on the Mental Development of Mankind*, transl. from the German by Peter Heath, Cambridge. ('Über die Verschiedenheit des menschlichen Sprachbaues und ihren Einfluß auf die geistige Entwicklung des Menschengeschlechts', *Gesammelte Schriften*, vol. VII, Berlin.)

Hurford, James (1987) *Language and Number. The Emergence of a Cognitive System*, Oxford.

Huxley, Julian (1963) *Evolution. The Modern Synthesis*, 2nd edn, London.

Itkonen, Esa (1991) 'What is a Methodology (and History) of Linguistics Good for, Epistemologically Speaking?', *Histoire Epistémologie Langage* 13/ 1, 51–75.

Jäger, Ludwig (1976) 'F. de Saussures historisch-hermeneutische Idee der Sprache. Ein Plädoyer für die Rekonstruktion des Saussureschen Denkens in seiner authentischen Gestalt', *Linguistik und Didaktik* 27, 210–24.

—— (1984) 'Das Verhältnis von Synchronie und Diachronie in der Sprachgeschichtsforschung', in Werner Besch, Oskar Reichmann and Stefan Sonderegger (eds) *Sprachgeschichte. Ein Handbuch zur Geschichte der deutschen Sprache und ihrer Erforschung*, Berlin and New York, 711–20.

Kant, Immanuel (1924/1978) *The Critique of Judgement*, ed. James C. Meredith, reprint, Oxford. (*Kritik der Urteilskraft*, ed. Karl Vorländer, reprint of the 6th edn 1924, Hamburg 1974.)

Keller, Rudi (1974) *Wahrheit und kollektives Wissen. Zum Begriff der Präsupposition*, Düsseldorf.

—— (1977a) 'Verstehen wir, was ein Sprecher meint, oder was ein Ausdruck bedeutet? Zu einer Hermeneutik des Handelns', in Klaus Baumgärtner (ed.) *Sprachliches Handeln*, Heidelberg, 1–27.

—— (1977b) 'Kollukutionäre Akte', *Germanistische Linguistik* 8, 1–50.

—— (1983) 'Zur Wissenschaftsgeschichte einer evolutionären Theorie des sprachlichen Wandels', in Thomas T. Cramer (ed.) *Literatur und Sprache im historischen Prozeß*, vol. 2: *Sprache*, Tübingen, 25–44.

—— (1984) 'Bemerkungen zur Theorie sprachlichen Wandels. (Eine Replik auf Dieter Cherubims und Peter Eyers Diskussionsbeiträge.)' *Zeitschrift für Germanistische Linguistik* 12/1, 63–81.

—— (1987) 'Der evolutionäre Sprachbegriff', in Rainer Wimmer (ed.) *Sprachtheorie. Der Sprachbegriff in Wissenschaft und Alltag*, Jahrbuch 1986 des Instituts für deutsche Sprache, Düsseldorf, 99–120.

—— (1989) 'Erklärung und Prognose von Sprachwandel', *Zeitschrift für Phonetik, Sprachwissenschaft und Kommunikationsforschung* 42/3, 383–96.

Kittsteiner, Heinz-Dieter (1980) *Naturabsicht und Unsichtbare Hand. Zur Kritik des geschichtsphilosophischen Denkens*, Frankfurt, Berlin, and Vienna.

Koch, Hansjoachim W. (1973) *Der Sozialdarwinismus: seine Genese und sein Einfluß auf das imperialistische Denken*, Munich.

Köhler, Reinhard and Altmann, Gabriel (1986) 'Synergetische Aspekte der Linguistik', *Zeitschrift für Sprachwissenschaft* 5/2, 253–65.

Koopman, Willem, van der Leek, Frederike, Fischer, Olga, and Eaton, Roger (eds) (1987) *Explanation and Linguistic Change*, Amsterdam.

Lass, Roger (1980) *On Explaining Language Change*, Cambridge.

—— (1984) *Language and Time. A Historian's View*, inaugural lecture, University of Cape Town.

—— (1987) 'Language, Speakers, History and Drift', in Willem Koopman, Frederike van der Leek, Olga Fischer and Roger Eaton (eds) *Explanation and Linguistic Change*, Amsterdam and Philadelphia, 151–76.

Levin, Jules F. (1988) *Computer Modelling Language Change*, mimeo, University of California at Riverside.

Lewis, David (1969) *Convention. A Philosophical Study*, Cambridge, Mass.

Lorenz, Konrad (1965) *Evolution and Modification of Behavior. A Critical Examination of the Concepts of the 'learned' and the 'innate' Elements of Behavior*, Chicago and London.

—— (1973) *Die Rückseite des Spiegels. Versuch einer Naturgeschichte des menschlichen Erkennens*, 2nd edn, Munich and Zürich.

Lüdtke, Helmut (1980) 'Sprachwandel als universales Phänomen', in H. Lüdtke (ed.) *Kommunikationstheoretische Grundlagen des Sprachwandels*, Berlin and New York, 1–19.

—— (1986) 'Esquisse d'une théorie du changement langagier', *La Linguistique* 22/1, 3–46.

Lyons, John (1968) *Introduction to Theoretical Linguistics*, Cambridge.

—— (1977) *Semantics*, vol. 1, Cambridge.

Mandeville, Bernard de (1732/1924) *The Fable of the Bees: or, Private Vices, Publick Benefits*, with a commentary critical, historical, and explanatory by F.B. Kaye, 2 vols, Oxford.

Martinet, André (1960) *Eléments de linguistique générale*, Paris.

Marx, Karl and Engels, Friedrich (1967) *Werke*, vol. 37, ed. Institut für Marxismus-Leninismus beim ZK der SED, Berlin.

Mauthner, Fritz (1912/1982) *Beiträge zu einer Kritik der Sprache*, vol. 2: *Zur Sprachwissenschaft*, reprint, Frankfurt-on-Main (1981), Berlin, and Vienna.

Mayerthaler, Willi (1981) *Morphologische Natürlichkeit*, Wiesbaden.

Maynard Smith, John (1972) *On Evolution*, Edinburgh.

Medewar, Peter B. (1959) *The Future of Man*, London.

Menger, Carl (1883/1963) *Problems of Economics and Sociology*, ed. Louis Schneider, transl. by Francis J. Nock, Urbana. ('Untersuchungen über die Methode der Socialwissenschaften und der Politischen Oekonomie insbesondere', *Gesammelte Werke*, vol. II, ed. Friedrich August von Hayek, Tübingen 1969 (1st edn 1883).)

Monod, Jacques (1969) 'From Biology to Ethics', *Occasional Papers of the Salk Institute of Biology* 1, La Jolla.

Mühlhäusler, Peter (1991) Review of *Sprachwandel. Von der unsichtbaren Hand in der Sprache*, by Rudi Keller, *Lingua* 84, 75–8.

Müller, Max (1864) *Lectures on the Science of Language*, 4th edn, London.

Nickl, Hans (1980) '10 Minuten vor dem Centre Pompidou', *Bauwelt* 40/41, 1789–92.

Nozick, Robert (1974) *Anarchy, State, and Utopia*, New York.

Nyman, Martti (1994) 'Language in the Guidance of the Invisible Hands', to be published in a forthcoming issue of *Diachronica.*

Osche, Günther (1987) 'Die Sonderstellung des Menschen in biologischer Sicht: Biologische und kulturelle Evolution', in Rolf Siewing (ed.) *Evolution. Bedingungen – Resultate – Konsequenzen,* Stuttgart and New York.

Paul, Hermann (1880/1970) *Principles of the History of Language,* transl. from the 2nd edn of the original by H.A. Strong, new and revised edn, reprint of the 1890 edn, College Park. (*Prinzipien der Sprachgeschichte,* 5th edn of the 1880 edn, Halle a.d.S. 1920.)

—— (1910) 'Über Völkerpsychologie', Rede anläßl. des Stiftungsfestes der Universität Munich am 25. Juni 1910, *Süddeutsche Monatshefte* 2, 363–73.

Peardon, Thomas P. (1966) *The Transition in English Historical Writing 1760–1830,* New York.

Popper, Karl R. and Eccles, John C. (1977) *The Self and its Brain. An Argument for Interactionism,* Heidelberg, Berlin, London, and New York.

Rádl, Emil (1909) *Geschichte der biologischen Theorien der Neuzeit,* vol. 2: *Geschichte der Entwicklungstheorien in der Biologie des 19. Jahrhunderts,* Leipzig.

Radnitzky, Gerhard (1983) 'Die Evolution der Erkenntnisfähigkeit, des Wissens und der Institutionen', in Rupert Riedl and Frans Kreutzer (eds) *Evolution und Menschenbild,* Hamburg, 82–120.

Rehbein, Jochen (1977) *Komplexes Handeln. Elemente zur Handlungstheorie der Sprache,* Stuttgart.

Ronneberger-Sibold, Elke (1980) *Sprachverwendung. Sprachsystem, Ökonomie und Wandel,* Tübingen.

Sapir, Edward (1921) *Language. An Introduction to the Study of Speech,* New York.

Saussure, Ferdinand de (1916/1974) *Course in General Linguistics,* revised edn, London.

Scheerer, Thomas M. (1980) *Ferdinand de Saussure. Rezeption und Kritik,* Darmstadt.

Schelling, Thomas C. (1969) 'Models of Segregation', *American Economic Review* 54, 488–93.

Scherer, Wilhelm (1874) *Vorträge und Aufsätze zur Geschichte des geistigen Lebens in Deutschland und Österreich,* Berlin.

Schleicher, August (1863/1869) *Darwinism Tested by Science of Language,* transl. by Alexander V.W. Bikkers, London. (Reprint in Konrad Koerner (ed.) *Linguistics and Evolutionary Theory,* Amsterdam and Philadelphia 1983.)

—— (1868) 'Eine Fabel in indogermanischer Ursprache', *Beiträge zur vergleichenden Sprachforschung auf dem Gebiete der arischen, keltischen und slawischen Sprachen* 5, 206–8.

Silbar, M. (1987) 'Cellular Automata', *Analog,* Sept. 1987, 68–80.

Slote, Michael A. (1989) *Beyond Optimizing,* Cambridge, Mass.

Smith, Adam (1776/1970) *The Wealth of Nations,* vol. I, reprint, London and New York.

Spencer, Herbert (1864/1966) *A System of Synthetic Philosophy,* vol. II, vol. I: *The Principles of Biology,* Osnabrück. (Reprint of the edn London, 1898.)

Stam, James H. (1976) *Inquiries into the Origin of Language: The Fate of a Question*, New York, Hagerstow, San Francisco, and London.

Stampe, David (1969) 'The Acquisition of Phonetic Representation', *Papers from the 5th Regional Meeting*, Chicago Linguistic Society, Chicago, 443–54.

Stein, Dieter (1988) 'Zur Philosophie des Natürlichkeitsansatzes im Bereich der Syntax', *Zeitschrift für Phonetik, Sprachwissenschaft und Kommunikationsforschung* 41/4, 471–5.

—— (1990) *The Semantics of Syntactic Change*, Berlin and New York.

Stewart, Dugald (1858/1971) *The Collected Works of Dugald Stewart, ESQ., F.R.SS*, vol. X, ed. Sir William Hamilton, Bart., Boston, Mass., republ. Farnborough UK 1971.

Stolz, Thomas (1990) 'Zur Ideengeschichte der Natürlichkeitstheorie: John Wilkins – ein unbekannter Vorläufer?', in Armin Bassarak, Dagmar Bittner, Andreas Bittner, and Petra Thiele (eds) *Wurzel(n) der Natürlichkeit. Studien zur Morphologie und Phonologie*, vol.IV Berlin, 133–44.

Strawson, Peter F. (1971) 'Meaning and Truth', in Peter F. Strawson, *Logico-Linguistic Papers*, London, 170–189.

Strecker, Bruno (1987) *Strategien des kommunikativen Handelns: zur Grundlegung einer Grammatik der Kommunikation*, Düsseldorf.

Strehlow, C. (1907–15) *Die Aranda- und Loritiaustämme in Zentralaustralien*, Frankfurt.

Süßmilch, Johann Peter (1766) *Versuch eines Beweises, daß die erste Sprache ihren Ursprung nicht vom Menschen, sondern allein vom Schöpfer erhalten habe*, Berlin.

Toulmin, Stephen (1972) *Human Understanding*, vol. I: *The Collective Use and Evolution of Concepts*, Princeton NJ.

Ullmann-Margalit, Edna (1978) 'Invisible-Hand Explanations', *Synthese* 39/2, 263–91.

Vanberg, Viktor (1982) *Markt und Organisation: Individualistische Sozialtheorie und das Problem kooperativen Handelns*, Tübingen.

—— (1984) '"Unsichtbare-Hand Erklärung" und soziale Normen', in H. Todt (ed.) *Normengeleitetes Verhalten in den Sozialwissenschaften. Schriften des Vereins für Sozialpolitik, Gesellschaft für Wirtschafts- und Sozialwissenschaften*, (Neue Folge, vol. 141), Berlin, 115–46.

Watzlawick, Paul, Beavin, Janet H., and Jackson, Don (1967) *Pragmatics of Human Communication. A Study of Interactional Patterns, Pathologies, and Paradoxes*, New York.

Weisgerber, Leo (1971) *Von den Kräften der deutschen Sprache*, vol. I: *Grundzüge der inhaltsbezogenen Grammatik*, 4th edn, Düsseldorf.

Whitehead, Alfred N. (1933) *Adventures of Ideas*, Cambridge.

Whitney, William Dwight (1867) *Language and the Study of Language: Twelve Lectures on the Principles of Linguistic Science*, London.

—— (1873) 'Schleicher and the Physical Theory of Language', *Oriental and Linguistic Studies*, New York.

—— (1875) *The Life and Growth of Language*, London.

Wildgen, Wolfgang (1985) *Dynamische Sprach- und Weltauffassungen (in ihrer Entwicklung von der Antike bis zur Gegenwart)*, Presse und Informationsamt der Universität Bremen.

Wilson, Edward O. (1975) *Sociobiology. The New Synthesis*, Cambridge, Mass. and London.

Wimmer, Rainer (1983) 'Metaphorik in der Sprachgeschichtsschreibung', in Thomas Cramer (ed.) *Literatur und Sprache im historischen Prozeß* (Vorträge des Deutschen Germanistentages Aachen 1982), Tübingen, 63–82.

Windisch, Rudolf (1988) 'Voraussagbarkeit des Sprachwandels', *Energeia und Ergon*, vol. II: in Harald Thun (ed.) *Das sprachtheoretische Denken Eugenio Coserius in der Diskussion* (1), Tübingen, 109–20.

Wittgenstein, Ludwig (1953) *Philosophical Investigations*, Oxford.

Wunderlich, Dieter (1976) *Studien zur Sprechakttheorie*, Frankfurt-on-Main.

Wurzel, Wolfgang Ulrich (1988) 'Zur Erklärbarkeit sprachlichen Wandels', *Zeitschrift für Phonetik, Sprachwissenschaft und Kommunikationsforschung* 41/4, 488–510.

—— (1989) *Inflectional Morphology and Naturalness*, Dordrecht, Boston, and London.

—— (1992) 'The Structuralist Heritage in Natural Morphology', in Hans-Heinrich Lieb (ed.) *Prospects for a New Structuralism*, Amsterdam and Philadelphia, 225–41.

Index

Aitchison, Jean 113
Alarcos Llorach, Emilio 98
Aristotle 40
articulative economy,
    development of language and
    122
Austen, Jane 3
Ayren, Armin 79

baby-talk 99
Bailey, Charles-James N. 114
Bally, Charles 124, 125
'because' 81, 82, 83
Beeh, Volker 42
behaviour, instinctive 40, 43;
    reason and 40, 43; rules of
    social 41, 42, 44
Bentham, Jeremy 142

'cause' 81, 82, 83
Charlie, story of 20–3, 25, 26–7,
    30, 35, 37, 85
Chaucer, Geoffrey 3
Chomsky, Noam 8; *Rules and
    Representations* 54; I-grammar
    55, 142; determination of
    human language and 79;
    natural language and
    autonomous syntax and 88; I-
    language and 126–33, 140, 142,
    149, 154, 159; language change
    and 153
communication 13, 14; human
    stages in learning 25–30;
    definitions of 45, 46; goals of

society and 86, 87, 88, 92;
    implications of 95, 96;
    intentions behind 5, 97–100,
    153, 154; optimal benefits
    between costs/benefits and 122,
    123; rate of social success and
    148, 149; small experiments in
    150, 152
conjectural history, Scottish
    philosophers' reflections on
    Mandeville's ideas and 35–8; *see
    also* Charlie, story of
conscious change, language and
    10, 12
Coseriu, Eugenio, *Synchrony,
    Diachrony and History* 79;
    language as a cultural object
    and 80, 142; language change
    and 81, 93, 95; synchrony and
    diachrony and 124, 125
cultural objects, historical
    development of 80, 142
cultural phenomenon, language
    as 52, 53
'cumulative process of small
    changes' 144
custom 41, 42, 43; language as a
    44; of law 45

Darwin, Charles 7, 47, 49;
    evolutionary theory and 83;
    social Darwinism and 142, 143
Dawkins, Richard, *The Selfish Gene*
    146; memes and 147, 148, 149
development of language,

articulative economy and 122
diachrony 123–6
dichotomies 39; examples of 40–6;
  Greek and arguments about
  others 46–53; Mandeville's
  escape route from 53; question
  of language made by people
  and 54–7
'displacement' 26
Dressler, Wolfgang U. 115
drift of language 112, 113, 114

Eccles, John C. 135
E-change 133
E-grammar 128
E-language 128, 132
Ellis, Alexander J. 19
Engels, Friedrich 18
englisch, disappearance of
  meaning 'angelic' from 80–3,
  124, 132; ecological conditions
  and 93, 94, 95; goal of
  understanding and 105; flight
  of homonyms and 156
epiphenomenon, language as 132;
  traffic jam as 138
evolution, and ideas it arouses 142
explanatory adequacy, language
  change and 152–9
Eyer, Peter 158

Fable of the Bees, The 32–4, 37
factors in determination of
  human actions 121
Fanselow, Gisbert 129, 130
Felix, Sascha 129, 130
Ferguson, Adam 35, 37, 57
'fitness' 145
flight of homonyms 156
footpath, story of 70–3
foreigner-talk 99
Frege, Gottlob 130
Frei, Henri 80
function, description of 85, 86, 88

garlic story, invisible hand
  explanation and 67, 72, 73
genesis of a structure 15, figs 1.1
  and 1.2 16, figs. 1.3 and 1.4 17

Gerard, R.W. 144
Germanic sound shift 158
Graham, Alma 76
Grice, Herbert Paul 29; language
  to influence others and 85;
  model and 91; what
  communicating means and 91
Grimm, Jakob 8, 122

Haakonssen, Knud 63
Hayek, Friedrich August von 32;
  human action and language
  and 35, 36, 39; rules for
  language and 40, 41, 44;
  traditions in language and 46;
  theory of language change and
  125, 158; views on social
  Darwinism and 143
Heringer, Hans-Jürgen, Germanic
  sound shift and 158
histories of language,
  displacement of words and 69
household of nature 142
human actions, determinants of
  121
Humboldt, Wilhelm von, on
  human beings and linguist
  organisms 49; phenomenon of
  third kind and 69; maxim of 99;
  language seen as producing by
  126; true definition of language
  and 142, 149, 154
Hurford, James 132, 133

I-change 133
I-grammar, Chomsky and 55, 140,
  127–33; conformance to
  convention and 131, 132
I-language 127, 132
individual competence, linguistic
  units and 147; hypothetical
  character of 149, 150; selection
  and communicative experiment
  in 152, 159
*An Inquiry into the Nature and Causes
  of the Wealth of Nations* 37, 45
instinctive behaviour 43
'intention', ambiguity in 10;
  different meanings of 11–13

invisible hand, Adam Smith and
37, 38; emergence of processes
of 90, 91, 92; seen as a cultural
model 144
invisible hand explanation 67–78;
Robert Nozick and 68; Edna
Ullmann-Margalit and 69;
essential attributes of 70, 71 72;
is often a conjectural story 72;
prognostic value of 73, 74;
surprise element in 75, 76;
usefulness of 77, 78; view of
historical explanations and 83,
84; a way to explain language
change 154, 155

Kluckhohn, Clyde 144

language, as a means to reach our
reason 23; as a way to facilitate
communication 25; as an
institution 52, 56; as a natural
phenomenon 52, 53, 56; as a
phenomenon of the third kind
57, 154, 155; morphology and
phonology of 116, 117, 122,
123; as a means of self-
presentation 89; stasis and
dynamics of 95–107; seen as an
activity 126; system of
conventions and 129; World 3
phenomenon and 133–40; a
way to influence others 153, 154
language change, advertising and
4; can be organistic or
mechanistic 5–9; decay and 7, 8,
69; causal, final and functional
explanations for 78–90;
invisible hand explanations for
67–78, 154, 155; Lüdtke's law of
108–14; naturalness and
114–23; necessary consequence
of how we use it 153; universal
tendencies and 117
language evolution, logical steps
in 24–30; what is implied by
141–6
language-making, conscious and
unconscious process of 78

languages, development of 47;
discussed as natural sciences 48;
discussed as historical sciences
50, 51; they are traditions 137
Lass, Roger, On Explaining
Language Change 74, 155, 156,
157; language change and 89,
96; laws of language 111, 112;
naturalness and language and
114, 115, 118, 119, 120;
reconstruction of change in
language and 120, 121; World 3
theory and 137, 138
Levin, Jules 100, 101; models of a
maxim 102 figs. 4.1 and 4.2, 103
figs. 4.3 and 4.4, 104 fig. 4.5
linguistic actions, maxims of 90–5
linguistic evolution 151; selection
and 151, 152
linguistic units, individual
competence and 147, 148
Lorenz, Konrad 7, 42
Lüdtke, Helmut 95, 105, 107; law
of language change and
108–14; optimum balance of
costs/benefits and 122, 123
Lyell, Charles 47

Malthus, Thomas 142
Mandeville, Bernard de 32, 35, 36;
Fable of the Bees 32–4, 37; escape
route offered by 46, 53;
paradox of 30–5, 37, 67, 76
map of isoglosses 101, fig. 4.6 104
Martinet, André 107
Marx, Karl 47
matrix, Popper's three worlds and
139, 140
Mauthner, Fritz 78
maxims of linguistic actions 90–5;
stasis and dynamics of 95–107
Mayerthaler, Willi 115, 117, 118
memes 146–8
Menger, Carl, Problems of Economics
and Sociology 65, 66; anticipation
of phenomenon of third kind
67, 125
Monod, Jacques 148
Mozart's Jupiter symphony 135, 137

Müller, Max, arguments used by 40, 47, 49, 50; criteria of 51, 52, 53, 56; invisible hand and 65; necessity and free will and 78, 79; struggle for survival and 142, 143, 146, 147

natural phenomenon, language as 52, 53, 56
naturalness, concept of 117; explanatory powers of 118, 119, 120; trends in language and 120, 121
'necessary', energy for talk and 108; meaning of word 109
Nickl, Hans 15
Nozick, Robert 68, 75

Origin of Species, The 7
Osche, Günther 85

Patton, Simon N. 143
Paul, Hermann 6; Principles of the History of Language 146; understanding change in language and 158
pejoration of expressions for women 76–7, 89, 114
phenomena of the third kind 57, 61–7; diagram of 62; example of 63, 64; language as 61, 145, 146
Philological Society of London 19
phonetic shrinkage 110, 111
planned change, language and 10
Plato 40
Pompidou Centre, Paris 15
Popper, Karl R., World 3 and 133–9, 154
'principle of fusion' 110, 111
'principle of quantitative compensation' 110, 111
process of historical evolution, conditions for 144–5, 146; memes and 146–8, 149
Prussian Academy of Sciences 23

Rádl, Emil, History of Biological Theories 76, 142

Rapoport, Anatol 144
rational behaviour 43
'real', definition by Popper 136
'redundancy management' 109
Ronneberger-Sibold, Elke 84
Royal Institute of London 50
rules, social 40, 41

Saltationist theories 85
Sapir, Edward 112
Satzklammer 141
Saussure, Ferdinand de 79; methodology and 123, 124; necessity for change and 153, 155
Scherer, Wilhelm 48
Schleicher, August, arguments of 46, 47; natural sciences and 48, 49, 50, 52, 53, 56, 142; social Darwinism and 142, 143, 151
Scottish School 36, 39
Sechehaye, Albert 124, 125
'signal-negentropy' 108
Smith, Adam 37, 38, 45, 68, 142, 143
Smith, John Maynard 141
social behaviour, in large societies 44
social Darwinism 142, 143
social rules 40, 41; benefits of 42; changes in 43
social success 87, 88; how to talk to achieve 106–7; memes and 148, 149
Société de Linguistigue de Paris 19
sociology of nature, Darwin and 143
Spencer, Herbert 47, 51
Stampe, David 115
Stewart, Dugald 36, 154
Strecker, Bruno 19, 154
struggle for life, words and grammatical forms and 143
Süßmilch, Johann Peter 19, 23, 24
synchrony 123–6

talk, energy necessary for 108;

redundancy management and
109; to be socially successful
106, 107
teleological process, language
evolution and 144, 145
theory of the footpath 70–2;
plausibility and 73
theory of the history of language,
explanatory adequacy and 159
theory of maxims, diachrony and
synchrony and 123–6
theory of naturalness 114–23
traffic jam out of nowhere, model
of 63, 64; phenomenom of the
third kind 137, 138
trichotomy of language 56, 57

Ullmann-Margalit, Edna 14, 69, 85

'universal grammar' (UG) 127,
129, 131, 132
'utterer's meaning' 29

Whitney, William Dwight,
arguments used by 46, 47, 48,
51; describes language as an
institution 52, 53, 56; how
process of language making
works according to 65, 78, 79
Windisch, Rudolf 156, 157
World 3 phenomenon: language
as a 133; other worlds and 134;
products of the human mind
and 135, 136; matrix to
illustrate 139, 140
Wurzel, Wolfgang Ulrich 115, 117,
118